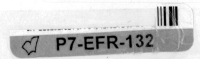

THE DEVELOPMENT OF PUBLIC SERVICES
IN WESTERN EUROPE
1660—1930

THE DEVELOPMENT OF
PUBLIC SERVICES IN
WESTERN EUROPE
1660– 1930

BY

ERNEST BARKER

ARCHON BOOKS
HAMDEN, CONNECTICUT — 1966

First Published 1944

Reprinted 1966 with permission
Oxford University Press
in an unaltered and unabridged edition

Library of Congress Catalog Card Number: 66-25182
Printed in the United States of America

PREFACE

SOME years ago the writer contributed a section to the fifth volume of *European Civilization*, a collective work published by the Oxford University Press under the direction of the late Mr. Edward Eyre. His contribution was one of the sections in Part IV of that volume—a Part entitled, 'A Study of the Modern State'. It followed a section on law and police; and it was designed to give some historical account of (1) systems of administration in the modern type of State ; (2) the treatment of person and property, by the methods used for raising armies and imposing taxes, and (3) the promotion of physical and mental welfare by means of State social services and State provision for education. It is that contribution which is here reprinted.

For a number of reasons—but especially for the reason that it marks the serious beginnings of modern science, in its application to human affairs—the year 1660 was taken as the starting-point of the account. For a number of reasons too (among them reasons of space), the account was limited to Western Europe, and to three of the countries of Western Europe—France, Great Britain, and Prussia. On this basis the use of a comparative method was naturally suggested; and the use of that method perhaps gives the account such value as it possesses. The result is thus a tentative and preliminary study, based on a comparative method, of the development of administration, and the public services generally, in the three main countries of Western Europe since 1660. The writer cannot but hope that others, following the same method (too little pursued), will illustrate with a deeper scholarship the parallelism and the interaction of the different phases of that development.

One lesson emerges. It is the lesson (briefly suggested at the end of the last chapter) that the different States of Western Europe 'have combined, however unconsciously, to promote the growth of a common European standard of administration and public service'. There is thus some hope for the future in

this record of the past. Perhaps there may also be some sugges-
tion for those who have to build the future, and whose business
it will be, in the coming years, to deal with the construction
of some common system of Europe.

No bibliography is appended. It would hardly be of service
unless it ran to great length; and the reader is asked to believe
that though few books are cited, a number have been read, and
used, by the author. He is also asked to remember that the essay
which he reads was composed before

Hi motus animarum et haec certamina tanta

which began over a decade ago. He may be surprised to find
an occasional reference to Germany as Germany stood before
1931. But perhaps he will not think that the essay is antiquated because it supposes a different Europe from the
Europe of 1943. It is the permanent past, not the fleeting
present, which will be the basis of the permanent future.

ERNEST BARKER

October 1943

CONTENTS

V. EDUCATION

THE DEVELOPMENT OF PUBLIC SERVICES
IN WESTERN EUROPE
1660—1930

CHAPTER I

ADMINISTRATION

§ 1. *General Factors and Considerations*

WE may begin the history of modern administration, some-what arbitrarily and yet with some reason, about the year 1660.

By that year England had decided that she would not follow the lines of an administrative absolutism, acting through the King's Privy Council and its ancillary organizations both central and local, but would be governed by the King-in-Parliament at Westminster, aided—or sometimes thwarted—by the local justices of the peace. In 1661 began the personal rule of Louis XIV; and during the next ten years, with the aid of Colbert, the inherited institutions of the past were shaped into the French administrative system which, modified and invigorated by Napoleon, still endures. In 1660 Frederick William, the Great Elector, secured for his troubled dominions in northern Germany a period of rest and reorganization; and though the history of Prussian administration is a long story, which began even earlier with Joachim Frederick's organization of a Council of State about 1600, and was to have large chapters written afterwards (by Frederick William I and Frederick the Great in the eighteenth century, and by Stein and his successors in the nineteenth), we may date its continuous progress from the reforms of that crucial period.

There is, of course, no single history of the growth of administration in Europe at large since 1660. Each country has its own system, determined by factors which are peculiar to itself. Apart from the factor of historic tradition, there are two others which deserve especial mention. One is the geographical —the conformation of a country internally, in point of extent and the ease or difficulty of communications; the nature of its position externally, according as it is free from or exposed to frontier problems. From this point of view there is a sense in which we may say that English administration (the administration of a small and compact country, bounded by an inviolable sea) is a simple thing compared with either Prussian or French. The other factor is the social—the nature of the system of classes on which administration has to act; the character of the social class from which administrators are drawn; their position and their standing in the social hierarchy. This is a factor of the first importance, which may particularly differentiate the administration of one country from that of another. But there are also some general threads which run through the inevitable differences. The prestige of the system of administration of one country may induce imitation, more or less conscious, in others. France was long a model in this way; and we may cite in evidence Frederick the Great's introduction of French revenue officers and his appointment of a Frenchman as head of the Prussian customs and excise. In more recent times Prussia herself, and since 1870 Germany at large, have played the same part: the organization of armies, the methods of education, and the planning of social services have all tended to be modelled on German patterns. Not only may the influence of a particular country inspire a general trend; a general movement of opinion may conduce to the same result. The *Aufklärung* of the eighteenth century, with its creed of superior benevolence and its utilitarian levelling rationalism, was the common inspiration of many rulers, in many countries, who sought to obey philosophy by becoming philosopher-kings, and to rationalize administration into the general uniformity of a clock-work providence. Russia, often an experiment ground for doctrine, affords an instructive example. The *nakás* of Catherine II which conveyed her instructions to the legislative commission of 1767 shows the age of 'enlightenment' carrying its torch to the farthest confines of Europe.

We must distinguish 'administration' from 'government'; and we shall do so best if we consider the relation of both of these terms to a third—'the State'. A State is a territorial society (generally, in our times, a territorial nation) organized as a legal association under and in virtue of a constitution. As such an association it observes a common law, and its members enjoy the rights and perform the duties which are guaranteed in that law. Government, in the broader sense, is the policy-determining branch of this association, which both declares and enforces, in harmony with its general opinion, the law to be observed, the rights to be enjoyed, and the duties to be performed. In the narrower sense, in which we identify it with the executive, it is the particular organ which is finally responsible for ensuring that the declared system of law, and of rights and duties, shall be an effective fact as well as a declared rule; in other words, it is the policy-enforcing organ. Administration is connected with government in this narrower sense of that term; but it is also distinct from it. It is the sum of persons and bodies who are engaged, under the direction of government, in discharging the ordinary public services which must be rendered daily if the system of law and duties and rights is to be duly 'served'. Every right and duty implies a corresponding 'service'; and the more the State multiplies rights and duties, the more it multiplies the necessary services of its ministering officials.

The administration, we may accordingly say, 'ensures the daily life of the State, and of its sub-divisions, by discharging the public services' which both require.[1] Where administration is concerned with the common services of the State at large, it is central; and from this point of view we have to consider its relations as a 'civil service' both to the government in the narrower sense of the executive, and to the legislative body to which that government is nowadays generally responsible. Where administration is concerned with the particular services of subdivisions of the State, it is local; and from this point of view we have to consider its relations both to the central administration and the central government behind it, and to the local elected bodies

[1] J. Barthélemy, *Le Gouvernement de la France*, c. ix, *ad initium.*

with which it is generally associated. (In some countries, as in France, the emphasis lies on the relation of local administration to the centre; in others, as in England, it lies on its relation to local elected bodies; in others, as in Prussia, there has been an attempt to link the local administration both with the centre and with local elected bodies in a sort of triple balance.) In regard to both central and local administration, a further question arises, which concerns their relation to the judicature and its courts. Are their actions cognizable in the ordinary courts, under process of common law; or do they belong to special administrative courts, which apply a special administrative law? England answers in one way; France and Prussia answer in another.

All these conceptions belong to the twentieth century. When we go back to 1660 we have to shed them and to think in different terms. The State is not regarded as a legal association, united in a common scheme of rights and duties which requires the discharge of public services. It is rather regarded from a number of different points of view, the inheritances of a long past, which present us with a blurred and yet living picture. If we place ourselves on the Continent, and more particularly in France, we may seek to suggest the salient features of this picture in, three propositions. (1) The State is a Family. 'The Family', Bodin had said, 'is the true source and origin of every Commonwealth.' The idea of the Family colours the general political scheme. The French king governs by a sort of *conseil de famille*, analogous to that of any French family, in which the queen-dowager and the princes of the blood will naturally sit. Government officials and the household staff run into one another: in particular, the expenses of government and the expenses of the household are confused, and there is no clear distinction between the family income of the 'father of his people' and the revenues of the State. (2) The State is Property, or, at any rate, the government of the State is property. Loyseau, a French jurist of the early seventeenth century, regards the king as 'owning' sovereignty in virtue of the prescriptive title of long possession. The matter goes farther than that: the king may actually own a large part of the territory of a State; and Frederick William I of Prussia, at the end of his reign (1740), drew from his royal domains little short of the same amount that he drew from public taxes. The conception of property covered even administrative office. The holder of office in France held a property for which he had paid, and which, subject to further payment, would descend in his family. Office in England in the eighteenth century, if it is not hereditary, is none the less property; and the rules about office come under the rules of the law of property. (3) The State is Society. More exactly, it is interlocked and intermixed with the play of society; and, instead of being a pure and impersonal legal structure which controls and adjusts that play, it is bowed and bent to its working. The confusion of State and Society is one which naturally follows on the identification of the State with Family and Property. It is a confusion which shows itself in various ways. Because the nobility has a special position in society, it must also have a special position in the State; and Louis XIV, though he is resolved that this position shall not be one of office and political authority, and though, as we shall see, he has his own idea of the State as incarnate in himself alone, is none the less concerned to adorn his nobles by pensions and gifts from public sources involving a species of 'social services' in aid of an indigent aristocracy. Again, and conversely, the class of officials, having a special position in the State, must have a special position in society; and accordingly the proprietary and hereditary official, organized in his *bureaux* and *compagnies*, attains the social dignity of belonging to the *noblesse*. Even the army is interfused with society. Companies are not raised or paid by the direct authority of the State. Members of the nobility and gentry become *entrepreneurs* for the purpose; and the army of the State is drawn into the general process of economic society.

This confusion of the idea of the State with notions of Family, Property, and general Society was generally characteristic of Europe about 1660; and the confusion still survived under Louis XIV, and into the eighteenth century. So long as it persists, it complicates and checks the development of a pure and

specific administration of public services. The disengaging of
the idea of the State, as a service-rendering organization for the
protection of rights and enforcement of duties, is the prior condition of such a development. There are two great landmarks
in the history of that disengaging. One is the institution of
absolutism, as it was inaugurated by Louis XIV. The other is
the proclamation of national sovereignty, as it was made in 1789.
Both of these movements, opposed as they are, agree in postulat-
ing a conception of the State as something separate and *sui generis*;
and it is in connexion with these movements that we can best
trace the general history of State administration.

§ 2. *The Administration of France under the ancien régime*

The pattern of absolutism was a pattern set by France. The
maxim ascribed to Louis XIV, *L'État, c'est moi*, has a profound
sense. Its negative implication is perhaps the more important.
The State is not to be confused with Family or Property or
Society; it is a self-subsisting unity on its own independent
account. The principle of that unity, however, is not to be
found in the idea of a legal association, united by the reasonable
wills of all its members, under a constitution which they have
given themselves; it resides in the idea of the reasonable will of
a single supreme Person who, as God's vice-gerent, connects and
constitutes a community under a scheme of order which he
creates, and for the realization of which he appoints a government and an administration. The *ministres d'État* who form
the government are therefore *his* ministers, executing his will
after learning it from him in personal conference; the *secrétaires
d'État* in Paris, and the *intendants* in the provinces, who form
the administration, are *his* chosen agents for discharging the
royal services which his will involves. This was the general conception of the new absolutism; and it was realized, as we shall
see, in Prussia as well as in France. The execution of this conception involved a revolutionary break with the past. It was
also to involve, in another and graver sense, a revolution in the
future.

It involved a break with the past. We may trace that break

both in central and in local administration. At the centre all traces of a family council disappear; and the government is conducted by the King in a *Conseil d'État* which only includes *les trois bourgeois*[1] who are his *ministres d'État*. This concentration is naturally accompanied by the growth of a central administrative bureaucracy, in order to cope with the demands of an over-burdened king and his still more overburdened ministers, and to realize the absolutist principle that personal will shall furnish a general scheme of order for the multifarious life of the whole community. The growth of a central administrative bureaucracy is not so much a break with the past (it is when we come to local administration that we find the true absolutist revolution) as an addition to what the past had bequeathed. France had long had four administrative secretaries, each with a territorial sphere covering a quarter of the *généralités*, or financial districts, into which the country was divided; and in the time of Richelieu it had become the custom to give to one or more of them some general interest, such as war or foreign affairs, in addition to his territorial sphere.[2] Louis XIV continued and developed the scheme; he made each of his ministers the head of a Secretariat, thus connecting government and administration; and he made the Navy a new general interest attached to the Secretariat held by Colbert. But two new developments also occur in his reign, which were both of permanent importance. One is the growth of large *bureaux* of officials attached to the secretaries—so large, we are told, that 'when the Court and the Government installed themselves at Versailles, the *bureaux* occupied exclusively the two long wings on either side of the fore-court.'[3] The other, and the greater, development is that of a new system of financial administration. The old office of Controller-General of Finances assumed a new position in the hands

[1] The 'Triad' which formed the government during the period of reconstruction between 1661 and 1672 consisted of Le Tellier, Lionne, and Colbert.

[2] A similar mixture of geographical spheres and 'functional' competence marks the two English Secretaries of State down to 1782. The Secretary for the North dealt with foreign relations with the northern States of Europe; the Secretary for the South was concerned with foreign relations with the States of southern Europe, Irish affairs, and internal administration.

[3] G. Pagès, *La Monarchie d'Ancien Régime*, p. 187.

of Colbert; it was equipped with a new 'treasury board', or *Conseil royal des finances*; and it drew into its sphere not only finance, but also agriculture, industry, commerce, and colonies. Nor was this all. The Controller-General was also, in view of his financial powers, in close touch with the local officials, themselves mainly concerned with matters of finance; and he was thus the Minister of the Interior as well as the head of the Treasury. In the hands of Colbert the office is connected, on the one hand, with the development of the system of *intendants*, and, on the other, with a State regulation of industry and commerce, by means of inspection and tariffs, which enabled absolutism to impress (or to attempt to impress) its own 'mercantile' scheme of order on the local and general economic life of France. In the hands of his successors the office of Controller-General was less important; but a powerful controller might at any time wield the influence, or even acquire the title, of *premier Ministre*.

In the sphere of local administration the break with the past was more revolutionary. The system of vendible and hereditary offices, of which we have already spoken, was deeply rooted in seventeenth-century France; and indeed its traces survive to-day, in an altered form, in the array of nearly 1,000,000 officials scattered over the soil of France. It was a system which encouraged the multiplication of offices, in order to increase the payments derived from grant and renewal; and it thus bred a disease which continued to be endemic in the French monarchy down to the Revolution. Almost all the administrative reforms of the *ancien régime*, it has been said, disguise financial expedients: they are only a veil for a new sale of offices; and the government of Louis XIV, no less than that of his predecessors, and also of his successors, descended to expedients of this character.[1] There was, indeed, one advantage to be derived from the multiplication of proprietary offices. It enabled the State to tap the elusive wealth of the middle classes. The King satisfied the bourgeois passion for the security and prestige of office—at a

[1] An edict of 1692 made municipal mayoralties into life offices which descended by heredity; another of 1704 extended the same rule to aldermen and other municipal magistrates; and in 1706 'alternative' mayors were instituted in order to secure a further profit.

price. But there were two great disadvantages. One was that so great a cloud of office-holders, not necessarily possessed either of personal ability or of technical experience, was not a fit medium for conducting the will of the absolute monarch to his subjects. The electric spark was lost in an opaque density. Another disadvantage was even graver. The numerous officers began to form a class and to organize themselves in corporations. This was a menace to the State, and the germ of a new feudalism. The 'treasurers of France', for example, who were concerned with the general management of taxes, formed a *collège* in each of the thirty-odd *généralités*, and maintained collective representatives at the Exchequer in Paris; the *élus*, who dealt with the repartition of the *taille* in those parts of France in which it did not fall to Provincial Estates, formed a *syndicat* at Paris about 1640. The danger became apparent in the beginning of the Fronde, in 1648, when treasurers and *élus* joined the Parliament of Paris, itself the greatest of all the colleges of officials, in an agitation against the monarchy. If absolutism was to be established, this danger must be removed. If the French monarchy had once broken the local power of the old feudalism by the aid of its officials, it had now to break the pretensions of these officials themselves, before they established their power as a new and corporate feudalism.

The instrument which it used for the purpose was the *intendant*, who became as essential to the local administration of France, from 1660 to 1789, as the *préfet*, his successor, has been since the days of Napoleon. The *intendant* of the *généralité* had existed, in an incipient form, before 1660; indeed the agitation of 1648 had been an agitation against his existence. He begins, under the government of Richelieu, and even earlier, as a commissioner, or *missus dominicus*, who is sent to inquire into the administration of justice, and into administration in general (including police and finance), for a given time, in a given district. We may compare him, in his beginnings, with an English eyre of the time of Henry II, inquiring into the justice and finances of a county; and indeed, in the days of Richelieu, he is generally selected, in much the same way as the justices in eyre, from a class of lawyers who have had both judicial and administrative experience in the capacity of *maîtres des requêtes*. We need not trace his development; it is sufficient to notice what he has become by 1670, and henceforth continues to be. He has ceased to be a temporary commissioner, who criticizes and reforms. He has become a new type of permanent administrator, entrenched in every *généralité*; holding a position which is not an 'office', in the old sense, but a power revocable at will; dependent utterly on the king and his ministers (and particularly on the Controller-General); the skilled and subtle instrument of the absolutist State. 'Know', said the Scotsman Law, at the beginning of the eighteenth century, 'that this kingdom of France is governed by thirty *intendants*.' It was the work of Colbert—a work perhaps begun in the days of Mazarin, under whom he was already engaged in the public service, and certainly pursued with a steady tenacity afterwards between 1660 and 1670—to settle the general position and the functions of the new officers. Virtual Minister of the Interior of an absolutist State, he needed them generally for his work; but he needed them particularly, as agents of economic inspection and control, for the mercantile policy of regulation natural to such a State. His *Mémoire* of 1663 (or 1664)[1] became the permanent charter of their functions: henceforward they had a general control of police, of justice, of finance; and charged, in addition, to verify and liquidate the debts of towns, they also became the local sovereigns of municipalities. Town as well as country; justice no less than police duties; the whole economy of the *généralité* as well as its finances—all fell under their sway: it was their business, the king wrote, to secure 'the observation of our edicts, the administration of civil and criminal justice and police, and all things else which concern the prosperity and security of our subjects'. We may notice particularly that they combined both justice and administration. This perhaps helps to explain the growth of the French system of administrative law: it also serves to explain the recruitment of the *intendants* from the ranks of the legal profession. We may also notice that, with their heavy

[1] The date is uncertain.

burden of duties, the *intendants* were naturally led to enlist the aid of a local bureaucracy, just as the central Secretaries had formed a central bureaucracy in Paris. They acquired their *subdélégués* and staff; they formed an administrative method and routine. Before this method and routine the relics of old local autonomy disappear, alike in the rural communes and the municipalities of France. All alike are *sous tutelle*.

This was the system which French absolutism built, in order to find a suitable instrument for realizing the personal will of an absolute monarch. It has been said of it that 'the administrative system is the real constitution'; and it is true that, so far as France had a constitution before 1789, that constitution was the structure and the routine of her administration. But this truth suggests a grave consideration. It is the ideal of absolutism that the absolute will should act freely, and come and go like a rapid lightning. It is the actual fact of an absolutist system that it issues in an administrative machine, through which all action necessarily proceeds. Not the flash of an electric spark, but the slow transmission of impulse, from a mainspring which may become relaxed through wheels which may become clogged, is the true analogy. So long as the impulse remains fresh and vital, and the administrative machine is receptive and runs easily, the ideal may be accommodated to the actual in a happy equilibrium between personal will and administrative routine. But the conditions are difficult to satisfy; and they were not long satisfied in France. In the first place, the monarchy lost its driving originality; it ceased to be distinct from the machine: it became identified with its own administration, and thus it was finally forced to pay the price of the defects of its agents. In the second place, acting only by way of administration, and making an administrative system the whole of the constitution, the monarchy excluded the great bulk of the community from any share in that constitution, and from any place in public life. Perhaps its worst fault was that it had deliberately rendered useless the nobility and landed gentry, which in England played so large a part both in local life and the central system of government; but it was the rising of the *bourgeoisie—*

the industrial, commercial, and professional classes who had also been left unenlisted in the constitution, and kept under administrative tutelage—which actively precipitated the Revolution.

Finally (and this is one of the heaviest counts) the absolute monarchy had stereotyped its will in one direction—that of external policy and war. Richelieu had once said to Louis XIII in 1630, 'Si le roi se résolvait à la guerre, il fallait quitter toute pensée de repose, d'épargne et de règlement du dedans du royaume.'[1] The French kings resolved upon war: they wedded absolutism to militarism: and they paid the price which Richelieu had foreseen. Because the will of the absolute sovereign ran to war, the administration became an administration controlled by the exigencies of war—directed to the financing of armies, and therefore directed, in its primary intention, to the extraction of taxes. It was not conscription, or the burden on men's lives, that weighed most heavily (the French army, down to 1798, was not a conscript army); it was taxation, and the burden on their purses. That burden weighed all the more heavily for two grave and sufficient reasons. The taxes were unequally distributed; both the nobility, as the price of their contentment with a splendid uselessness, and the official classes, as part of the price of their work, were in practice exempt from the incidence of any direct taxation. Again they were uneconomically collected, and inadequately controlled when they were collected. French administrators, in spite of their ability and their experience, had not learned the secrets of financial administration.

§ 3. *The Administration of France since the Revolution*

The result was the coming of that 'revolution in the future' which, from the early years of the eighteenth century, had always threatened the absolute monarchy. Absolutism fell in 1789, and it fell with a resounding crash. It had sought, indeed, to disengage the idea of the State, but it had never entirely succeeded: it had still permitted social privileges to invade the political system; and so far as it had succeeded it had

[1] Cited in G. Pagès, op. cit., p. 106.

disengaged a State which was military rather than civil and concerned with external relations and power rather than with internal order and *le règlement du dedans*. A new conception of the State now appeared in the doctrine of 'national sovereignty'. The nation, and not the king, is *l'État*; the general will of the nation, and not the absolute will of the monarch, is sovereign. We might expect this doctrine to obliterate the past, and to issue in a new system of administration, under which a national parliament would control the central administrative services, and local elected bodies would govern in the sub-divisions of the nation. This was, indeed, the original intention and tendency of the Revolution, with its policy of a weak central executive and its sweeping measures of local decentralization; but France soon halted and checked in this course—partly under the threat of internal confusion and discord, and partly under the pressure of foreign wars. Nor could the past be shed as easily as the revolutionaries had dreamed. A system of administration which had worked since the time of Colbert, and had settled into the habit of the nation, could not be readily scrapped. It was not scrapped. France retained the administrative machine of the past, but gave it a new motive power. She provided a new mainspring, but left all the wheels.

The new motive power, or mainspring, was the new-born will of an emancipated nation, conceived as a 'person' with a *moi commun*—a collective 'person' which vindicated sovereignty, and the right to bear the style of *l'État*, from the individual and single person of the absolute monarch in the old régime. This was a further stage in the disengaging of the idea of the State. The Revolution, if it made a new confusion between a personal nation and the impersonal State (thus enthroning the personal will of a national *moi* instead of the impersonal rule of a common law), at any rate abolished the old absolutist theory which, while seeking to disengage the State from property-rights and social interests, had proceeded to treat it as the property and interest of a single individual. But while it made this advance, and thus produced a theory of democracy, the Revolution left its new theory of democracy curiously united with the old prac-

tice of bureaucracy. As Woodrow Wilson wrote, in the days
when he was still a professor, 'it removed all the foundations of
French politics, but scarcely any of the foundations of French
administration'.

The conjunction of democratic government with bureaucratic
administration still marks the political system of France. The
conjunction becomes less strange when we remember the position, the prestige, and the permanent influence of Napoleon.
Napoleon was the bridge which united democracy and bureaucracy. At one end, the bridge rested on the foundation of the
national will; the emperor, four times endorsed by a national
plébiscite, was 'the first representative of the nation'; if Louis XIV
had simply said, 'I am the State', Napoleon could say, more
subtly but with greater force, 'I am the nation, *and therefore* the
State'. At the other end, the bridge rested on a controlled and
centralized administration, as the absolutism of Louis XIV had
done before; but, while Louis could only delude himself into
thinking that he controlled his basis, Napoleon, with his far
greater genius for organization and direction, was actually in
control.   He was the successor of Colbert rather than of
Louis XIV; or rather he was the successor of both—at once
the indefatigable organizer of administration and *Le Roi Soleil*.

Napoleon's reorganization of France was completed, in all its
main lines, in the four and a half marvellous years which run
from November 1799 to May 1804—the years which gave France
three successive 'Constitutions', a Civil Code, and a new administration. In the new administration, with which alone we
are here concerned, the elements of cardinal importance are the
Conseil d'État and the system of *Préfets*. The Napoleonic *Conseil
d'État*—the precursor of the present *Conseil d'État*, which is one
of the most remarkable institutions of France—is entirely different from the *Conseil d'État* of Louis XIV. That had been the
government, through which Louis XIV and his chosen ministers
had controlled the central administration and the whole of
France. Napoleon's government was simply himself, with the
aid of departmental ministers whom he consulted separately and
controlled entirely. His *Conseil d'État* was a body distinct from

the government, and yet closely connected with its working. It may be defined, as Professor Barthélemy has defined the modern *Conseil d'État*, as 'le conseil des jurisconsultes et techniciens qui assiste le gouvernement dans la solution des problèmes les plus élevés de l'administration générale'.[1] Under Napoleon it consisted of some forty-five salaried councillors—lawyers, administrators, and men of civil and military experience. It was the great and trusted organ of the régime, constantly at work, and constantly consulted, so that in 1804 it handled 3,365 *affaires*.[2] It produced the *Code civile* of 1804; but two of its activities, which are still of importance to-day, deserve more especial mention. It was concerned with drawing up ordinances relating to public administration, just as to-day it draws up *règlements d'administration publique*; it was also concerned with the settlement of administrative disputes, and with the judgement of cases in which the officials or services of the State were involved, just as to-day it is still the supreme organ (subject only, in some degree, to the 'Court of Conflicts') in all cases of administrative law.

Parallel to this central system, in which Napoleon governed through his ministers and their staffs with the consultative aid of the *Conseil d'État*, ran the system of local administration instituted early in 1800, in which the *préfet*, himself under absolute central control, governed through his sub-prefects and the mayors of communes with some measure of deliberative aid from local councils. The *préfet* is the heir of the *intendant*, superimposed on the new revolutionary unit of the department; but he is an heir fitted into a new world of administrative conceptions. A famous phrase, used by the astute Rœderer in introducing the new system of local administration in 1800, resumes the essence of these conceptions. 'Administrer est le fait d'un seul: délibérer est le fait de plusieurs.' The history of local administration in France, since 1800, has been a progressive commentary on this phrase. As it was applied by Napoleon, and as it has been progressively applied since, it involves a new doctrine of separation of powers, which regulates the area of local administration. (1) There is the power of *active* administration,

---

[1] Op. cit. c. ix.   [2] The number now runs to some 30,000.

exercised by the individual prefect, who controls the individual sub-prefects and the mayors of communes, but is controlled by an individual superior in Paris. (2) There is the power of *deliberative* administration, which belongs to bodies of persons. This is a power which, if we are to understand it properly, we must subdivide in turn; for there are refinements within refinements. (*a*) There is deliberative administration proper, which is concerned with the *action* to be taken on the issues assigned to its scope and belongs to local deliberative bodies such as the General Council of the department. Of this it is sufficient to say that the issues assigned to local deliberation under the Napoleonic system were very few (mainly relating to the repartition of central taxes and the voting of local rates), and that little scope was left to free election in the recruitment of the local deliberative bodies which were vested with these exiguous powers.[1] (*b*) There is what may be called consultative administration, which is concerned with the *advice* to be given on matters of administrative dispute, and is thus really concerned with administrative law. This belongs to the nominated *conseil de préfecture*, with its salaried members; and the function of this body thus corresponds, on a small scale (and the scale is very small in comparison), to one of the two main functions of the central *Conseil d'État*.

The Napoleonic system has undergone great changes. With Sedan there finally disappeared any idea of the emperor as 'the first (and only) representative of the nation'. National will now controls the administrative machine of France, not through an imperial incarnation, but through a national parliament—a national parliament which, in no small measure, has inherited the mantle of Louis XIV and Napoleon; which always completes its full term of four years (never being, in fact, dissolved before the end of its term), and is steadily in session for most of

[1] Little as was the deliberative power left to local bodies under the Napoleonic system, that which was left to central bodies, in the central scheme of government, was even less. The First Consul started, at the beginning of 1800, with three deliberative bodies (Senate, Legislative Body, and Tribunate), in addition to the consultative *Conseil d'État*. Within half a dozen years, he virtually dispensed with them all, and 'governed by means of *Senatus Consulta*, which he sent straight to the Senate for ratification, or by decrees drawn up for him by the Council of State' (*Camb. Mod. Hist.* ix. 109).

each year; which controls the ministers of the Government almost as drastically as its predecessors, partly through its standing committees, which always confront and may often check a ministry, and partly by its frequently exercised power of dismissing ministers; which finally—through the pressure exerted by deputies on ministers, and in turn transmitted by them to prefects—can even exert an informal control of local administration. The Council of State, as it was organized by Napoleon, persists, and it still enforces administrative law; but by a beneficent change in its recruitment, and in the spirit of its working, it now uses its powers to compel officials to the adequate performance of public services, to punish any 'excess of power', to protect the liberty of the citizen against administrative abuse, and, in brief, to prove that an administrative court may be *le meilleur juge contre l'État.*[1]

The Napoleonic system of local administration still controls the daily life of France; but it too has undergone changes. The local deliberative bodies were made elective a century ago; and the number of issues assigned to their deliberation and control has been extended by the law of 1871 relating to departments, and by the law of 1884 in regard to communes. Administration none the less remains centralized. The prefect is still an official nominated and controlled by the central government; and if elected bodies in departments and communes have received a larger scope of 'deliberative administration', they have also been kept under regular *tutelle*, both in their decisions and their expenditure, by the pressure of the central administration and the local prefect. The centre has given measures of local autonomy with the left hand, and imposed measures of *tutelle* with the right; and one of the problems of France is still the problem of decentralization. Its solution would seem to be connected with the future of 'regionalism'. It is argued that only a unit larger than the department—a unit which is a whole region—can successfully administer, on the basis of decentralization and local

---

[1] J. Barthélemy, op. cit. c. x, § ii *ad finem.* See also, on the present working of the French system of administrative law, A. Esmein, *Éléments de droit constitutionnel,* 8th edition, vol. i, pp. 568–73.

self-government, great services such as high-roads and railways, public health, and public assistance.[1]

§ 4. *Prussian Administration before 1806*

Another system of administration which has been developed since 1660, and developed, like the French, in close connexion with absolutism, is the Prussian. Nourished on the hard and exacting soil of north Germany, in the midst of poverty and under the conditions of a stern struggle for political existence and expansion, Prussian administration has shown a severe austerity and a Spartan character. The Hohenzollern rulers, from the Great Elector onwards, made themselves hard-working 'servants of the State'; they drilled their officials and agents into an equal rigour of service; and they gradually created an administrative staff which outstripped even the French. 'Conscription' was long the keyword of Prussia. Her kings conscripted the lives of their peasants; they conscripted the services of their nobles; they also conscripted themselves. Prussian absolutism almost redeemed its nature by its impartial impersonality. It was the rule of a categorical imperative of duty rather than of a personal will; but the obedience exacted was obedience not to the moral law of practical reason, but to the political law of 'reason of State'—the exigencies of Prussian frontiers and the demands of the crucial position of Prussia in central Europe.[2]

The Great Elector (1640–88), inheriting the Council of State instituted by his predecessor, Joachim Frederick, to check the pretensions and resist the intervention of the old feudal estates, had laid some of the foundations of Prussian administration. He had established a body of officials throughout his dominions, chosen freely by himself from his various territories and the other German States; he had begun the establishment of a

---

[1] The same argument may also be applied, *mutatis mutandis*, to England. Decentralization has long been with us; but many of our counties and county boroughs are not sufficiently large to handle adequately the varied problems of education, public health, and public assistance with which they are now confronted.

[2] The idea of *Einkreisung*, as it came to be called in our own days, is far older than the twentieth century, and almost seems to be inherent in the geographical position of Prussia.

standing army, which was to become the core of his State; he had introduced (apparently on the French model) an urban excise and a monopoly of salt to support his civil and military system; he had founded a postal system, which not only helped to link his dominions, but extended its benefits beyond their frontiers.[1] But it was his grandson, Frederick William I (1713–40)—the second of the Hohenzollerns to bear the title of King of Prussia, assumed by the Great Elector's son and successor in 1701—who stamped his mark most deeply on the Prussian State. He was the Corporal-King who made his State a 'polity of officers'. 'I am', he said once (and his saying is the Prussian version of *L'État, c'est moi*), 'the Finance Minister and the Field Marshal of the King of Prussia.' He was particularly resolved to be the Field Marshal of a great Prussian army; but, while he willed that particular end, he also willed, and prepared, a general system of means.

The army came first; and it was to be an army of the old Roman pattern, demanding the last measure of devotion from all. The king gave himself to its call; he regarded himself as a republican, vowed to the army of the republic; he charged his son in his testament, 'You must *work*, as I have always done'. He declared, in an early edict, that all the young men of town and country, under the natural and divine order of things, were bound to serve him with their lives; and, in particular, he laid a heavy burden on the nobility. They were to serve for life as officers in the army; they were to be a nobility of army service, justified by the performance of State duty, as well as a nobility of social privilege. At that price he was even willing to enhance their privileges; they were exempt, except in east Prussia, from direct taxes; they were favoured against other classes, and made into a ruling caste.

This was the foundation; and on it Frederick William I erected a method of finance and a system of administration to correspond with its needs. The method of finance which he followed was not so much that of addition to income as of rigorous

[1] In this respect his postal system has its analogies with the Prussian Zollverein of the nineteenth century.

reduction in expenditure; and he was sparing and Spartan enough not only to pay his way, but also to accumulate a considerable balance. It was impossible, however, to attain this result without careful management of the Crown domains (which produced nearly one-half of his revenue), or without a proper system of officials to secure the full yield of the taxes; and Frederick William I overhauled the administration accordingly. He created in Berlin a single General Directory, as the central administrative department; he instituted, in each province, a chamber of War and Domains to administer the province; and he appointed, as commissioners under these chambers, Councillors of Taxes (*Steuerräthe*), who were analogous to the French *intendants*, and were set to control, and practically to administer, a group of towns or a single town of large size. Municipal autonomy disappeared in Prussia before the *Steuerrath*; but the economic prosperity of the towns, as well as the royal taxes, benefited by his work.

This was a system which lasted till the Prussian collapse after Jena and the reorganization which followed that collapse. Rigorous as it was, and even despotic, it had two great merits. Unlike the *ancien régime*, in France, it enlisted the nobility in the service of the State and made them useful, even if it also made them militarist in spirit and privileged in position. At the same time, and though it suppressed local liberty in the process, it gradually trained a class of professional administrators, devoted to Prussia (Frederick William I would never station an official in his native province, lest he should forget his primary loyalty), and equally devoted, with the zeal of a *Fachmann*, to their profession. Frederick the Great made few changes in his father's system. The nobility continued to be an enlisted and utilized nobility; they were compelled to take commissions in the army, but they alone were qualified for commissions; and on these terms they were regarded by Frederick as 'the foremost class in the State', and aided by him to establish provincial banks of agricultural credit for the improvement of their estates. The Prussian administration had to endure the introduction of a French superintendent, and nearly 200 French officials, in the department of customs and excise; but this compliment to French administration, if it annoyed the native officials at the time, was also a stimulus to their activity. The accessions of territory due to Frederick's wars were another stimulus; and here we touch a consideration which is of primary importance in the history of Prussia, not only at this time (and indeed even before this time) but also long afterwards.

Prussia was not, like France or England, a formed State, with a contiguous and homogeneous territory. Deeply as this affected her general history, it perhaps affected, most of all, the history of her administrative development. A steadily growing State, in a constant process of formation down to 1866, she needed an able and skilled administration to digest the growth. A scattered State, with territories that eventually stretched from the Rhine to the Vistula, she needed such an administration equally to bind her scattered units together. There was no unity of a common tradition; there was not, until the end of the eighteenth century, the unity of a common body of law; still less was there any common representative body (the Prussian *Landtag* was only created in the middle of the nineteenth century); the one unity was that of a common administration. We may almost say that the Prussian State was a transcendent administrative entity (with an army at its core) superimposed on the living and homely fact of scattered provinces and divergent provincial sentiments. From that point of view we begin to understand the German political philosophy which has grown on the basis of Prussia—the philosophy of a transcendent State, a mind above individual minds, which adjusts social differences and corrects particularist antinomies in a serene and elevated solitude.

The officialdom of Frederick William I's days had been a rough instrument; and his successor could jeer at the councillors of the chambers of War and Domains as mainly fit for the gallows. But its standard steadily rose. Frederick's own enlightenment, his French models, and the demands of his arduous reign, did something. The Prussian universities, such as Halle and Königsberg, where a training in law could be gained by the future administrator, or an ethical theory such as that of Kant could be imbibed, did more. The codification of a common body of Prussian Law (*Allgemeines Preussisches Landrecht*), begun under the inspiration of Frederick the Great, and achieved under his successor in 1791, was at once a triumph of the Prussian service and a buttress to its professional dignity and honour. When Prussia went down at the battle of Jena, in 1806, there was an able administration ready to join hands with the enlightened members of the service nobility in rallying round the king, and in creating a new Prussia to meet the strain and the stress of new and troubled times.

§ 5. *Prussian Administration from 1806 to the Present Time*

The old Prussia, as it had taken shape under Frederick William I, was a personal absolutism, half redeemed by its impersonal devotion to duty of State, and governed by two instruments—an army-service nobility, whose members were collectively a dominant caste and individually the privileged owners of a serf peasantry; and a civilian bureaucracy, which had not only supplanted, in each province, the old privileges and liberties of the provincial estates, but had also been made to engulf municipal liberty—and that on a soil on which, from the Middle Ages onwards, the town and its traders and merchants had always held a high position.[1] It was the work of the Prussian reformers, headed by Stein, who had joined the Prussian service at the end of Frederick the Great's reign, to purge the old Prussia of its defects and, while leaving absolutism still the main basis of the State, to attach new and emancipated elements of the population to its support. Between 1807 and 1811 serfdom was abolished; peasant proprietorship was inaugurated; and one of the blots on the old system was removed. In 1808 a scheme of municipal reform was passed which, while it left the State still in general control of the towns, instituted

---

[1] The German towns, alike in the old and settled south, and in the newer and colonial lands of the north and east, have always been a bulwark of German civilization. To this day many of the towns of Germany, as centres of local culture and of social experiment, play a much greater part in national life than the provincial towns of France or England.

a remarkable system of municipal government, combining the professional element (dear to Prussia) of paid burgomasters and paid councillors with provision for the local election of this element and the co-operation of local elected bodies in its activity. In this way another blot on the old system was removed; and a new spring of voluntary activity was added to Prussian administration. But Prussia would not have been Prussia unless these reforms had also been accompanied by a reform of the army which was her core; and indeed these reforms were adjusted to, and connected with, a new and revolutionary plan of military organization. The essence of this plan was a new conception of the army, not as the drilled and disciplined instrument of a Royal Field Marshal, but as the expression of a nation in arms and 'the union of all the moral and physical energies of the nation'.[1] It is easy to see, in the light of this conception, how peasant emancipation and municipal liberty were linked with the general scheme.

To complete the picture of the revolution wrought in Prussia after 1807 we must add the reform achieved in the nature and action of the central government in Berlin. The old Council of State instituted by Joachim Frederick had grown in numbers, but it had lost in importance what it had gained in size. The General Directory, created by Frederick William I to serve as the central administrative department, had begun during the latter part of the eighteenth century to split into various departments, or embryonic ministries, but it had done so in a haphazard way. The king was the only link; but the king himself, from the reign of Frederick the Great onwards, had further complicated matters by introducing a cabinet of private advisers, distinct both from the old Council of State and from the General Directory and its departments. A new system and simplicity were introduced into the confusion when, in 1808, five definite ministries were instituted, and the heads of these administrative departments were united in a *Staatsministerium* which advised the king and acted as his government. The

[1] On the general character of this military reorganization, after 1807, see below, p. 46

private cabinet thus disappeared; the Council of State survived, and attempts were made to regulate its composition, and to increase its powers, with a view to making it the organ of general survey and co-ordination. Fortunately, perhaps, for Prussia, these attempts failed. It was a Parliament, rather than a Council of State, however the latter might be reformed, which was needed to complete the structure of Prussian government.

Thus was achieved the Prussian revolution of 1807–10. It was a revolution curiously unlike the French—a revolution not directed against the administration, but achieved by it; a revolution which left absolutism almost intact, but increased the efficiency of its methods of government, and gave it something of a national basis in a national army, an emancipated peasantry, and a liberated townsfolk; a revolution which reformed gymnasia, and founded the University of Berlin,[1] in addition to reforming the civil and military machinery of State. The Prussian monarchy, saved by its own Roman conception of duty to 'the Republic' and by the qualities of its army-service nobility and its trained administration, had stepped almost at a bound from the Louis XIV circle of ideas, in which the king is *ipso facto* the State, into the Napoleonic conception, by which the ruler is only identified with the State because he has first been identified with the nation. But it would be a grave mistake to exaggerate the degree of national unity in Prussia in 1810. Prussia had not gone through the purging and uniting fires which had made one people in France from the old heterogeneous French society; and the Prussian *Volk* after 1810, if in moments of crisis it was one, continued to show class-cleavage and social differentiation. The Prussian king seemed to be at one with his people; but it was a people divided against itself, and he was particularly allied with one of its divisions—the noble and military class which immediately surrounded his throne.

Not until the *octroyé* constitution of 1849, revised and accepted in 1850 by the two chambers which it instituted, was

---

[1] On the educational reforms of Prussia at this period, see below, p. 84

there any form of parliament for Prussia as a whole.[1] When a general parliament for Prussia was at last instituted, it was not a parliament of the type common in Western Europe, either in its composition or its powers. In its composition it still reflected the old medieval class system of estates, and still bore traces of the old Prussian conception of the State as an 'officer-polity', in which an army-service nobility was the ruling caste. Not only was the Upper House predominantly composed of the landed nobility; the House of Representatives was also constructed on a three-class system (with electoral classes determined by the amount of their taxable property) which gave a preponderant representation to the wealthier elements of the population. In its powers, again, the Prussian parliament, far from being the mainspring of government, was only, at best, a brake. In Prussian theory down to 1918, and largely in Prussian practice, *der Träger der Staatsgewalt* is still the king; it is he who 'carries the person' and exercises the authority of the State; and if he is to some extent controlled by a parliamentary 'organ' (which he has himself created by his *octroi* of 1849), he has at his disposal another 'organ' in his administration, and he and this 'organ' will generally carry the day in a conflict—the more as he also controls the army. Throughout the nineteenth century, in spite of the reforms made at the beginning and the constitution granted in the middle, the absolutist conception of the State is still evident in Prussia. Partly under the shelter of that conception, and partly in the strength of its own fine training and expert experience, the administrative class remains a powerful element in the State. When we think of the various factors which are here combined and dovetailed together—absolutism; parliamentarianism (itself a combination or dovetailing of a quasi-medieval three-class system with a

---

[1] Provincial 'Estates', on the old medieval class system, had long existed in many of the provinces; and in 1823 the Prussian government had resuscitated and extended these Estates, and given them some innocuous powers of petition, deliberation on local affairs, and discussion of laws affecting their province. A clumsy attempt was made, between 1841 and 1847, to create a form of central parliament by combining the various Provincial Diets; but a new central *Landtag* was first created by the Constitution of 1849.

modern bicameral system); a powerful civil administration, university-trained and office-experienced; an army and an army staff even more powerful—we cannot but marvel at the elaborate adjustment of the Prussian State.[1] We might almost call it 'a student-polity'—a polity contrived and balanced by the subtlety of scholars, anxious to find and balance the best in all possible elements. How simple in comparison (and yet, in some ways, still doctrinaire) is the new Prussian constitution of 1920, which declares that *der Träger der Staatsgewalt ist die Gesamtheit des Volks*; which makes this single and unitary people express its will directly by popular vote (in initiative, referendum, and elections), and indirectly through its appointed organs, especially the Diet or parliament; which, finally, makes the Diet elect the minister-president, and the minister-president nominate the other ministers.

The same balancing of different elements, and the same policy of 'student-creation', appears in the organization of the local government of Prussia, as it was elaborated by the *Kreisordnung* of 1872, regulating the circles which formed the basis of local government in every province, and by the *Provinzialordnung* of 1873 which was gradually extended, by 1888, to all the provinces except Posen. The problem of municipal government had already been settled, in its main lines, by Stein (himself a student as well as an administrator): something had also been done, at the same time, to settle the problem of rural government; but that settlement had now to be brought into conformity with the character of the new Prussian constitution of 1849–50. Gneist studied, and depicted for Prussia, the history of English local government, and the nature of its connexion with parliamentary institutions; and the transformation of the Prussian system of local administration, as Jellinek says, 'was

[1] Mention should also be made, in order to complete the enumeration of the various factors, of the Economic Council (*Volkswirthschaftsrath*), a sort of consultative 'Economic Parliament', instituted, in the latter part of the nineteenth century, to consider laws or ordinances affecting larger economic interests, and consisting of members appointed by the king, mainly on the nomination of economic organizations. It is the precursor of the *Reichswirthschaftsrath* in the Weimar Constitution

achieved, to no small extent, under the influence of the German theory of English self-government'—though, as he adds, the result was by no means a copy of the English system, inasmuch as the still earlier influence of French principles of organization, as well as the surviving influence of native institutions, were also contributory forces.[1] In truth the new system combined something of the French *intendant* and *préfet*, and something of the English justice of the peace and his quarter sessions, with something of the old Prussian Chambers of War and Domains and the old Prussian system of provincial estates.

It was a balanced and dovetailed structure, analogous to the balance and adjustment of the central system. The cadres of the structure were the twelve provinces; each of these was divided, first into administrative districts, controlled by a *Regierungspräsident* with a professional and salaried board, and then into units of self-government called circles; and finally the circles were divided into rural and municipal communes (*Gemeinde*), which formed the ultimate units. Running through these various cadres we may trace a number of principles or elements. In the first place, there is the element of 'active administration'. This was generally conducted on a collegiate basis, by salaried professional boards; and here we may notice a difference from the French system, which entrusts active administration to a single person. On the other hand, especially in the administrative district, the president of the active administration held a position of primary importance, analogous to that of the French *préfet*; and like the French *préfet* he represented, and obeyed, the central administration and government. In the second place, there is the element of 'deliberative administration' by locally elected bodies. This element appeared in the circle (though not in the district, which was entirely the sphere of active administration); but the elected body, or diet, of the circle was restricted in composition, being constituted on a sort of three-class system which gave weight to the landed gentry, and it was also restricted in powers, having by its side a professional administrative board which served

[1] G. Jellinek, *Allgemeine Staatslehre*, 3rd edition, pp. 630–1.

the president of the administrative district. In form, the diet of the circle had some resemblance to the old quarter sessions of the English justices of the peace, in their office of governing body of the county; but in reality it had far less power. If Prussia attempted a sort of triple balance between local administration, administration at the centre, and locally elected bodies, the balance dipped heavily towards the dependence of local administration upon the central authority. Finally, we come to the principle or element of administrative law (*Verwaltungsrecht*). In Prussia, as in France, the official acts of administrative officers were reserved for administrative courts, of which there was one in the circle and another in the administrative district, with a final court in Berlin. Administrative law, while it may be used to protect the liberty of the citizen, must also tend to enhance the position of the administrator. The local administration of Prussia down to 1918 was essentially a domain of the powerful and professional administrator, admirably trained and admirably skilled—but also regulating his district admirably, and admirably regulated himself by the central government. . . .[1] Here, we may note, as in its scheme for the organization of central government, the new Prussian constitution of 1920 breaks with the past. It proclaims for civic communities (*politische Gemeinden*), and for groups of such bodies, the right of self-government (*Selbstverwaltung*); it proclaims a system of provincial autonomy, under which provinces are to administer their own affairs by organs of their own, and the range and scope of such affairs is to be increased; and it enunciates the new principle that officials shall be free to belong to local elected bodies, and to join, as elected members, in their activities.

§ 6. *The Administration of England in the Eighteenth Century*

The history of the development of administration in England is very different from its history in France and Prussia. Administration in England, since 1660, has not developed in the single frame of an absolutist or one-man State; it has developed

---

[1] Municipal government, with its system of committees, enlisting the services of a large number of citizens, stood in some respects apart from the general scheme.

over the varied ground of a generally active political community in which the landed gentry of the counties, the citizens of corporate towns, and even trading bodies (such as the old East India Company) have all played a part in the general conduct of a common political life. While France was insisting, by the Revocation of the Edict of Nantes, on unity of religion, England was becoming a home of Free Churches, which influenced deeply her political life, alike by the genius of their inner spirit and by the challenge which they steadily offered to all policies of conformity. While France was seeking to control all economic life by a central controller-general and his *intendants*, England was practising a system of voluntary economic activity, which promoted more than any other cause the rapid growth of her commerce and industry.[1] Finally, while the nobility and gentry of France were powerless before the *intendant*, and, destitute of local authority, were content to exact dues from their peasantry in order to lead a satellite life at Paris, the English nobility and gentry were masters of Parliament at Westminster, and the governors, through quarter sessions, of their shires. But the converse of this picture, and a converse which may well inspire us with modest reflections, is that while France (and, we may also add, Prussia) 'made a science of the service of the State', England 'considered it a task for intelligent amateurs'.[2]

The peculiar development of England depends upon a number of factors. An island country, it has enjoyed external security; a compact country of small extent and easy communications, it has not needed administrative pressure to give it internal cohesion and unity. Its activity has not been an activity of war, except by sea; and England has not known, as France and Prussia have known, the effects of military exigency in producing an organized administration to cope with the task of providing not only recruits and taxes, but also the general system of

---

[1] England, it is true, followed a mercantilist or protectionist system in the eighteenth century. But any real attempt at State-protectionism had ended with Charles I; and English commerce, while claiming legislative protection, largely went its own way. See G. Unwin, *Studies in Economic History*, pp. 28, 341.

[2] Professor Pollard, in the *Camb. Mod. Hist.* x. 353.

internal control which a great army needs as its basis. The last native dynasty ended with Elizabeth; and it was difficult for Englishmen to regard even their Scottish, and still more their Hanoverian kings, as incarnations of the English State. Nor was England ever imbued with the logic of that system of 'estates'—of separate and divided classes, with separate and conflicting interests—which in other countries gave absolutism both its opportunity and its justification, at once permitting it to play on social divisions, and enabling it to plead that, by bringing the divided interests under its own control, it was securing the unity of the State. We still talk of the estates of the Realm; but we have never allowed the 'estates' principle really to control our national life. Socially, there have always been bridges between the different elements: the younger sons of the noble class have passed into the class of commoners (itself combining both rural freeholders and the urban owners of mercantile wealth); and conversely commoners have passed, by way of successful pursuit of the law or of business, or from the position of large rural freeholders or squires, into the ranks of the nobility. Politically, the same system of links has also held good; parliament has not been a parliament of estates, but of 'houses'; and while one house has united a lay nobility with an upper clergy the other has combined the knights of the county with the burgesses of the town. We have had neither the useless but privileged court nobility of the French monarchy, nor the privileged but utilized army nobility of Prussia.

Administrative absolutism was attempted for a time in England, between the accession of Edward IV in 1461 and the supremacy of the Long Parliament in 1641. The French model was before the eyes of the English kings; and in the organization of the Privy Council and its administrative committees, in the development of the position and powers of the Secretaries of State, in the creation of local commissions (such as those for the North and for Wales), they attempted to follow the model.[1]

[1] Professor Hatschek, in his *Englische Verfassungsgeschichte*, repeatedly emphasizes this French influence, down to the days of Charles II and Clarendon; cf. pp. 416 sqq., 423 sqq., 426 sqq., 433–4, 438–9.

But the attempt fell on stony ground. Neither the geographical position nor the social structure of England demanded such a system; nor was the nature of English society such as to make Englishmen long patient of it when it was actually attempted. By 1660 the die had been cast in favour of other methods. What was restored in 1660 was not Monarchy but Parliament; and when James II ignored the verdict the lesson was driven home by the revolution of 1688. Henceforth the theory of the English State is a theory not of the administrative absolutism of a king, but of the legislative omnipotence of a parliament—a parliament which, indeed, includes the King as well as the Lords and Commons, but moves steadily through the eighteenth century to the signification of Lords and Commons, as it moves again, from 1832 onwards, to the signification of the Commons alone. Under the conditions of the eighteenth century we may speak of this Parliament as absolute. The sovereign, which 'is called also the legislature of the State', Paley holds, has a power which 'may be termed absolute, omnipotent, uncontrollable, arbitrary, despotic'; and Burke similarly speaks of 'the unlimited and illimitable nature of supreme sovereignty', as Blackstone also writes of 'a supreme, irresistible, absolute, uncontrolled authority'.[1] From this point of view the legislature appears as the *Träger* of an absolute *Staatsgewalt*; and if we wish to heighten the picture we may say that it not only legislates, but also virtually appoints, and actually controls, a 'government' which consists of an *Ausschuss* of itself that goes by the name of Cabinet.

But we must not exaggerate this absolutism. In the first place, there is also the 'Crown'; and, though the nature of the Crown is mysterious, 'administration' is done in its name. The 'government' may be, in some sense, a legislative *Ausschuss*; but it is also a body consisting of His Majesty's ministers, or at any rate of his principal ministers. In the second place—apart from the limits imposed on the legislature by other parts of the constitution, in which we have to include a great judicature, with its

---

[1] Paley, *Principles of Moral and Political Philosophy*, book vi, c. vi; Burke, *Speech on American Taxation*, vol. ii, p. 433 (in Bohn's edition); Blackstone, *Commentaries*, vol. i, p. 49.

own historic tradition of law, as well as the Crown, its ministers, and their subordinate officials—we must remember that, in and by itself, Parliament simply legislates, and its absolutism only expresses itself in the form of legal enactments. None the less, and when we have made these allowances, the legislature still remains the core and kernel of the State. It has given the Crown its title, by the Revolution settlement; it has generally become the central force of the State. It follows that the activity of the State will be largely an activity of the legislature. It follows on this in turn that there will be less importance attached to central administration. It follows on this, again, that local government will tend to proceed on its own orbit, with little reference to the central administration, and under the direction (so far as there is direction) of the central legislature. In a word, we shall have a central parliament of nobility, gentry, and their allies in the mercantile class: we shall have a number of local parliaments, or county legislatures, of much the same composition; and between the two the idea and practice of administration, whether central or local, will be largely elided.

This was indeed the general character of the English State in the eighteenth century. It was a State of legislators, and therefore of amateurs. It was not devoid of central administration, and it was far from devoid of central administrative departments, in which offices of profit might be enjoyed; but these departments were peculiar, alike in the class of officials whom they employed, and in the nature of the powers which those officials exercised. Office was a property, for which a consideration was paid at the time of acquisition; and officials recruited on this basis were not so much professional administrators, after the Prussian pattern, as *rentiers* who were anxious to draw good dividends from the investment they had made, and who were drawn themselves from the propertied classes which were able to make the necessary investment. Each department had a 'fund', constituted mainly of the fees which it received (and which it naturally did its utmost to increase); the 'patentee' at the head of the office, acting as a sort of *entrepreneur*, took care of his share of the profits, and left the subordinates to fare as best they could. Such a system did not ensure capacity; and in any case the powers and position of the departments left little room for its development. The departments were for the most part boards, meeting round baize-covered tables; and their administration had the characteristics of administration by boards. The boards multiplied; each of them 'deliberated'; one of them 'referred' an issue to another; rapidity of administration was lost. It was a more serious matter that these boards had seldom a real power of direct administrative action. They issued warrants to act, or instruction about action; they were not themselves the organs of action, or even the inspectors of its efficiency. Secluded in their offices, and among their papers, they did not touch the citizen directly; and the Napoleonic principle of 'active administration' was a thing which was almost unknown.

Under these conditions there was little if any control of local administration by a central administrative authority. There was no 'Ministry of the Interior': before 1782 there was not even a separate Home Office; until that date internal affairs had been assigned, along with Irish matters and foreign relations with the southern States of Europe, to the southern Secretary of State. Local administration was in the hands of the justices of the peace of each county and the municipal councils of each borough. The justices of the peace were particularly powerful; the administration of the poor law, which under the Elizabethan system had shown some signs of parochial independence, was brought entirely under their sway by an Act of 1691 which subjected the parish overseers to their directions; and the so-called 'Speenhamland Act of Parliament', of 1795, shows how the 'college' of Berkshire justices, meeting at the Pelican Inn near Newbury, could initiate its own policy of public assistance as if it were a sovereign body. So far as there was any central control of local administration, it was not administrative control, but either legislative or judicial. On the one hand, Parliament, in the way of Private Bill legislation, settled a host of problems of local administration (as, for instance, the paving and lighting of streets), and, incidentally, appointed a host of special authorities, under the name of Improvement Commissioners, in connexion with its settlements. On the other hand, the courts of law, by the procedure of *certiorari* and *quo warranto*, kept local authorities (and administrative authorities in general) within the bounds of law appointed by the legislature; and the rule of law, which on our English interpretation includes the absence of administrative courts and jurisdiction, was thus secured. Apart from these restrictions local self-government, as it existed down to the era of change which began about 1830, was a paradise of autonomy. There were theorists who held that this was one of the ways in which 'the balance of the constitution' was preserved. Local self-government must balance central government, no matter what balance of different functions and organs that government itself contained, if the general liberty of the nation was to be safe.

§ 7. *The Reforms of English Administration in the Nineteenth Century*

A new period in the history of our central administration begins with Burke's speech on economical reform in 1780; a new period in the history of local administration, which also involves a crucial change in English conceptions of central administration and its relations to local authorities, begins with the Poor Law Amendment Act of 1834. The movement which began with Burke, continued with Chadwick, and is still at work, has given us a new system of central administration, and a new Civil Service. The multiplicity of boards has gone; a more logical articulation of administrative functions, and the creation of administrative departments for each of these functions, has taken its place. The Home Office is still the residuary legatee of internal administration; but by its side (apart from the all-seeing Treasury) there is a Ministry of Health, concerned with local government, and some eight other departments, all concerned in their various ways with the administration of internal affairs. The officials of all departments are a professional class, paid and pensioned directly by Parliament from the general revenues of the State (though it was not till the middle of the nineteenth century that this system became universal); and since 1870 the principle has been established that they should be generally recruited by open competition.

An effective instrument of civil administration has thus been created, with a regular organization of different departments for its working; and with this development (which indeed was intended to serve that purpose) the English system of central administration has undergone a revolution of scope and function. The legislative State of the eighteenth century could not cope with the needs of the industrialized England of the nineteenth century. A vastly increased population, redistributed by 'industrial transference', vexed by industrial problems, and raising on every hand grave issues of adjustment, demanded a more flexible instrument of regulation than parliamentary Private Bills and judicial rulings. Beginning with the Poor Law Amendment Act of 1834, which introduced central administrative control in the sphere of public assistance, we have gradually progressed a long way in the direction of the administrative State. Parliament is still active; but the volume of administrative activity has increased in a far greater proportion. In the main, the administrative activity of the State is concentrated in London. We have nothing analogous to the French prefect or the Prussian *Regierungspräsident*. State administration, as it appears outside London, mainly takes the two forms of inspection (by the local 'inspectors' of the central offices), and of financial criticism and check, which is all the more necessary as the State contributes large grants to the expenditure of local bodies.[1] But the scope and the functions of administrative activity in London to-day might amaze even Chadwick, the vigorous champion, in 1834, of central administration on the model of France. The central administration not only administers actively in the sense of discharging public services in accordance with the policy of government and in obedience to the expressed will of Parliament; it also legislates, and it also judges. It legislates

[1] The central government of the State, as Mr. Sidney Webb wrote in 1910, 'has successively "bought" the rights of inspection, audit, supervision, initiative, criticism and control by the grant, in aid of the local finances, of annual subventions from the national revenue'.

by 'orders', as authorized by Parliament thereto, in order to
supplement and execute in detail the general provisions of its
Acts. It judges, in the sense that it decides, if and so far as it is
authorized by Parliament thereto, contentious issues arising
under a variety of Acts, more particularly those relating to
social matters such as housing and insurance. In this sense
England is beginning to know 'administrative law'; and the old
idea of the universal 'rule of law', administered by the Common Law judges, is losing some of its rigour.

A parallel and connected revolution has also occurred, during
the century since 1832, in the nature of local administration.
The old system of amateur government by the general competence of the justices of the peace in the county, subject to such
central control as Parliament and the courts of law could
enforce, has been gradually eliminated; and at the same time,
but with far greater rapidity, the old system of municipal
government and slow-moving civic oligarchies has also been
abandoned. The reform of the national electoral system in
1832 naturally led to the reform of the local electoral system
in towns and also to the creation of a new electoral system in
counties. The Municipal Corporations Act of 1835 introduced
into a new industrialized and urbanized England a new method
of municipal government by elected councillors which was at
once more democratic and more effective. The Poor Law
Amendment Act of 1834 instituted elected Boards of Guardians
in the area of each Poor Law Union to take over the control of
poor relief from the justices of the counties. For many years
subsequently it seemed as if each new service which the State
undertook, whether it were the provision of communications,
or of sanitation, or of education, were destined to result in the
creation of a new *ad hoc* elected body, with its own special area
and its own separate electoral system. Highway Boards were
instituted; Urban Sanitary Districts were created; School Boards
were erected under the Education Act of 1870. In so far as the
old functions of the justices were transferred, or new functions
were assigned, to local elected bodies, the result might be argued
to be democracy. It might also be argued to be polyarchy; and

it was at any rate obvious that the government of great urban communities, and of great urbanized areas, could hardly prosper when each new purpose was assigned to a new and separate authority. The Act of 1889, which erected some sixty county councils, and gave to the councils of some sixty county boroughs the powers of county councils, not only completed the elimination of the old governing powers of the justices in their quarter sessions; it also provided a new focus for the development of a new system of 'integral' local government. Two subsequent Acts have contributed to that development since 1889. One was the Education Act of 1902, by which the councils of counties and boroughs took over the local control of public education from the School Boards: the other was the Local Government Act of 1929, by which they succeeded to the Boards of Guardians in the control of poor relief. The local council has now become the general local authority; and it has added a new and important element to the system of local government by acting, for the purposes of education and poor relief, through special committees on which co-opted members of the general public, representing experience and knowledge in those fields, can sit and vote by the side of its own elected members.[1]

Two other changes have accompanied these large and sweeping developments.

In the first place, local government has developed its own administrative staff, appointed by local elected bodies, and acting under their general control. Locally, as well as centrally, the cult of the amateur has yielded to the profession of the administrator; and county education officers, to take only one example, have become important officials, 'balancing' (in a new way) the officials of the Board of Education in Whitehall. In the second place, as we have already had occasion to observe, the new growth of local government and local administration from below has come into a new relation, and formed a new

---

[1] This method of acting through special committees which included co-opted members had long been used in the municipalities of Prussia. Lord John Russell, in an abortive education bill of 1853 intended for boroughs, had already proposed that each borough council should set up a school committee, and that half of the members of the committee should be co-opted.

system of connexion, with the growth of central administration from above. The central Parliament and the central courts of law have still their say in the sphere of local government; but it is now the various departments of the central administration which are most vitally connected with its operations. We have already seen how this connexion has been established, and how the departments have 'bought' their rights of inspection and criticism by the provision of grants in aid. It only remains to add that the general nature of the connexion is neither central control, nor decentralized local autonomy, but rather co-operation—co-operation between central departments and local authorities in realizing the declared will of Parliament and furthering the declared policy of government.[1]

CHAPTER II

CONSCRIPTION

§ 1. *Military Organization in its relation to Political Ideas*

WE have traced, in three crucial instances, the modern development of that system of administration, central and local, which secures the due discharge of public services. We have now to sketch the development of the methods by which the State exacts from its members the performance of two duties inseparably connected with its services—the duty of providing armed forces to render, in the last resort, the service of maintaining order and peace, and the duty of providing a revenue to support the cost of that and of all other services. When we have dealt with the methods by which the State has sought to secure from its members the performance of those two duties, it will remain to deal with the methods by which it has also sought to secure for its members the enjoyment of two rights.

---

[1] The writer, in this summary sketch of the development of modern administration, has confined himself to three main types; which seemed to him representative —the French and Prussian, as different examples of the general Continental trend; and the English, as representing a peculiar trend which during the nineteenth century (along with the English Parliamentarianism with which it was connected) began to be studied and imitated on the Continent.

They are rights which are inseparably connected with its services; and indeed their enjoyment is the very object and purpose for which some of the main services of the State exist. One of them is the right to the service of education. The other is the right to those 'social services', as they have come to be called, which consist in the maintenance of life and health by the provision of adequate housing, of healthy conditions of factory work, of compensation for injury incurred in the course of work, of insurance against sickness and unemployment, of assistance in the event of destitution, and of pensions for old age.

The size and composition of an army, and the nature of its position in the general system of a State, mainly depend on two factors, one of which is changing and the other constant. The constant factor is the geographical situation of a State, and the problem of its frontiers. The changing factor is the political idea, or set of ideas, which dominates the State at any given time. The political idea dominant in France down to 1789 (and even afterwards, though it assumed a new and Napoleonic form after the Revolution) was the idea of absolutism, which made the absolute monarch claim not only to dominate the State, but to be its very essence and incarnation. Under a system of absolutism the activity of the State tends to become an activity of war. War, in itself, is the greatest of games for an absolute ruler; and it also offers to the 'owner' of a State a chance of increasing the area of his 'ownership'. The army, under these conditions, is next to the throne; and the business of administration, as we have already had occasion to observe, becomes the business of providing and equipping an army. But absolutism is faced by an inherent defect, even in the very matter which lies nearest to the heart of an absolute ruler. It cannot, in its own logic, attempt to create a national army. It may appeal on occasion to the nation, as Louis XIV did in 1709, when he was confronted by demands from his enemies which wounded France as well as her king; but its normal army will be an army determined, not by the energy of a national will, but by the extent of its own power to compel the services of its subjects. A national or civic army—an army

which is the 'people in arms', or the *levée en masse* of the nation
—must in the long run require a national or civic polity.

There is a paradox in this matter which cannot but suggest
mixed reflections. Absolutism in its nature tends to be bellicose; and yet its nature imposes a limit upon the armies which
it can raise. It seems difficult to think of a whole nation as
bellicose by nature, though it may well be so in a moment of
national excitement; it seems particularly difficult to think of
nations as bellicose when once they have developed a democratic practice of government, which involves the pacific process of discussion and debate upon all issues, including the issues
of peace and war. And yet vast national armies, of unprece-
dented dimensions, have accompanied the growth of national
self-consciousness, and even of democratic institutions. It may
seem to many a tragedy of history that such a growth should
be accompanied by such a shadow. But there is a logic in the
connexion; and the shadow is not entirely black. An army
which embodies the whole of a nation is from one point of
view a 'conscript army', compulsorily enrolling its hundreds of
thousands; and that is the point of view which is natural to
English thought. But such an army, from another point of
view, is a 'civic militia' in which all the members of a civic
community voluntarily join in order to serve the commonwealth not only by vote and tax, but also by a greater gift.
This is the point of view which, in the course of the nineteenth
century, came to be natural to French and German thought.
It is not a point of view to be summarily rejected. A civic force,
whose members must spend themselves in war, is not necessarily 'militarist'; indeed, it may be the opposite. It is still
difficult to pass a final judgement on the system of a 'nation in
arms', because the historical development of that system has
not been pure and unalloyed. Though it is a system which is
not in the logic of absolutism, and though it belongs, on the
contrary, to the idea of the nation and national sovereignty,
it was none the less connected with absolutism in its beginnings, alike in Napoleonic France and in Hohenzollern Prussia.
The movement of national ardour, in the first decade of the

nineteenth century, fell under the glamour of a modernized absolutism; and it flung its gift of a national army at the feet of a French emperor and a Prussian king. Times have changed; but national self-government is still a new thing on the Continent of Europe. We are only some sixty years removed from the fall of the second Napoleon, and less than a third of that time from the fall of the last king of Prussia. The fates have not yet pronounced on the conjunction of a national army with national self-government, or on the permanent results of that conjunc-tion.

§ 2. *The French and Prussian Armies down to the end of the Eighteenth Century*

The French army of the *ancien régime*, down to 1789, was a professional force, without being altogether a profession. A confusion between State and Society still persisted in France, and the army of the State was infected both by social privi-leges and by economic processes. The officers were members of the nobility who had bought their commissions; and the raising and payment of troops was a sort of economic under-taking, on the basis of a contract made with the government, in which the officers might make a profit on their men, or might possibly incur a loss. It was the general system of the time; and it was equally current in England, where it lasted into the nineteenth century. Louvois, the War Minister of Louis XIV, left the system much as it stood, and he contented himself with insisting that the men for whom the officers drew pay should actually be on the strength, and with seeking to improve the higher command and the technical equipment of the troops. The army grew in numbers to suit the ambitions of his master; and from this time onwards France had a large standing army, such as had not been seen since the days of the Roman Empire. On the eve of the Revolution the regular army numbered 173,000; and it could be raised, in time of war, to 211,000. This was a voluntarily enlisted force, one-sixth of which was composed of foreigners; and, though it was large, it was not altogether out of proportion to the size of the

French population, which now numbered something over 25 millions. In addition there was a militia for home defence of 55,000 men, which could be raised, in time of war, to 76,000. The number of men annually required for the militia was only 10,000; and these were raised by a form of conscription, irregularly applied, and attended by numerous exemptions. Both in the raising of the regular army by voluntary enlistment, and in the use of a modest form of conscription for the militia, the French system was much the same as that of contemporary England; and indeed the French army, down to the Revolution, only differed from the English in its size.[1]

The Prussian army, in the form which it had assumed by the middle of the eighteenth century, was peculiar; and its analogies, so far as any existed, were rather with Russia than with western Europe. The Great Elector, by the year 1660, had gathered an army of 25,000 men. His successor Frederick I raised the number to 40,000; and he formed in addition a militia, which, however, disappeared with his death in 1713, and was not renewed until the *Landwehr* was embodied against Napoleon in 1813. (The absence of a militia, and an entire reliance on regular troops, is one of the peculiarities of eighteenth-century Prussia.) It was the achievement of Frederick William I to raise the standing army during the course of his reign to 80,000 men (half natives and half foreigners), and to make that army, in drill and discipline, incomparable in Europe. It was the further achievement of Frederick the Great to double the army which his father had already doubled before him, and to test and temper it in years of battle. By 1789 the regular army of Prussia was 162,000 men, rising to 250,000 in time of war, as compared with the French army of 173,000, which could be increased in war to 211,000 or (if the militia be included, at its war strength of 76,000) to 287,000. When we reflect that the population of Prussia in 1789 was less than one-third of that of France, we cannot but recognize that the

---

[1] It is worth remarking, in this connexion, that the population of England and Wales was only about one-third of that of France at the end of the eighteenth century.

achievement was great—and that it was terrible. Napoleon, who once said of himself that he could use up 25,000 men a month, had nevertheless some justification for the proposal which he made to the Tsar, in 1809, that they should 'do Europe the service of abolishing the system of enormous standing armies begun by Prussia'.

We have already remarked that Prussia, as a new State in process of formation, with far-stretched and scattered terri-tories, was compelled to find unity in and through a super-imposed administration; and we may also add that, for just the same reason, she was also compelled, and compelled even more, to find unity in an army, where the noble officers and the impressed peasants of all her provinces could serve together. But it was the will of a Hohenzollern king, as well as the pressure of impersonal forces, which made Prussia the successor to Rome, as Rome had been the successor to ancient Assyria. Frederick William I is an important figure in the history of Prussian administration; he is a still more important figure in the history of the Prussian army. A sturdy 'Republican' of an antique type, he offered to the Republic (as he conceived it) a full measure of military devotion.

He made a great standing army which differed from other armies, not only in being far greater, in proportion to the popu-lation on which he could call,[1] and not only in being more truly standing, because it was kept embodied in peace, but also in being supported by an accumulated war treasure, which Freder-ick the Great largely increased in spite of his wars. Voluntary enlistment was originally the method employed for raising the army, but recourse was soon had to impressment in recruiting the native troops, who numbered 40,000; and eventually, with-out being introduced by any law or edict, an informal method of conscription began to be applied. The captains of companies introduced the practice of enrolling the lads of their districts at an early age, giving them some token of enrolment, and call-

---

[1]. The army of Frederick William I stood at 80,000 when the population of his territories was estimated at only 2,000,000. It was 1 in 25 of the population, when the army of France was about 1 in 150.

ing them to the colours when they were considered ready for
service. The burden fell particularly on the peasantry of the
country-side; but the officers sought to extend it, in order to
sell exemptions, to the middle classes in the towns. It was not
a system of national service, either in the extent of its application or in the idea by which it was inspired; it fell particularly
on one class, and its aim was not to nationalize the army, but
to arm and drill as much of the nation as possible. But nobles
as well as peasants were compelled to serve, and the officers
who enrolled the peasantry had themselves been also virtually
enrolled. The officer class in Prussia belonged to a more severe
school than the officer class in contemporary France.

§ 3. *The History of Conscription in France and Prussia since the beginning of the Nineteenth Century*

The emergence of a national army, in the proper sense of the
word, is connected with the French Revolution, which brought
the conception of the nation into the foreground of general
politics. The nation, conceived as a 'person' with a *moi commun*,
had come by 1789 to be regarded as the State; it was natural
that it should also come to be regarded as an army. This was
the logic of the Revolutionary doctrine; but it is instructive to
notice how tentatively and with what variations of policy the
most logical of nations has followed that logic. It would be a
mistake to think that the old professional army of France
disappeared with the Revolution. It became the army of the
Revolution; its fine non-commissioned officers, and some of the
best of its officers, passed into the Revolutionary service; ten
of the marshals of Napoleon had been privates in the reign of
Louis XVI. Nor, during the earlier years of the Revolution,
was the old method of voluntary enlistment dropped. Apart
from the *levée en masse* of 1793, originally proposed for the whole
of the people of France, but reduced by Danton to the more
modest dimensions of a compulsory enlistment of Frenchmen
between the ages of 18 and 25, the army continued to be
recruited on a voluntary basis down to 1798. In that year the
Directory, harassed by wars, passed the Law of Conscription,

and thus introduced, for the first time in Europe, the principle that the regular army (as distinct from the militia) should normally be composed of conscripts. All unmarried Frenchmen between the ages of 18 and 25 were henceforth made liable to service, and an annual law was passed to determine the number actually required in each year. The Law of Conscription was intensely unpopular; and of the 200,000 men required, in the first year of its application, the Directory only succeeded, after months of pressure, in actually raising less than 40,000. But Napoleon, when he became First Consul at the end of 1799, inherited an instrument which his organizing ability and the prestige of his victories enabled him to turn to good effect. If we include the members of the National Guard, or civic militia, which still continued to exist under the Consulate and Empire, though it was only one-seventh of the total military force, we find that the annual levy amounted, during the four years of the Consulate, to 52,500; during the first four years of the Empire (1804–7) to 107,500; during the next five years (1808–12) to 166,600; and in the single desperate year of 1813 to 1,140,000. It was some alleviation of the burden, to the nation at large, that it fell on the unmarried; that a system of drawing lots made its incidence fall with some sort of rough justice; and that it was possible for those on whom the lot fell to provide substitutes—at a price. But the burden remained; and there were constant attempts to evade its terror. If Frederick William I's agents had been man-hunters in search of recruits, Napoleon's police had to perform the same office.

With the Restoration the law of conscription was abolished; and France went back to a standing army, on a footing of 240,000 men. Voluntary enlistment soon proved inadequate; and it had to be supplemented by the old method of drawing lots. The Orleans Monarchy, in its general movement towards the principles of the Revolution, reorganized the army on the principle of national service or general conscription; but the law of 1832 allowed a conscript to send a relation, or a paid substitute, in his place. Napoleon III, by a law of 1855, ingeniously made the principle of national service yield the

practical result of a professional army. He allowed the conscript who did not wish to serve, instead of sending a paid
substitute, to pay a sum directly into the *Caisse de la dotation de
l'armée*; and the funds thus secured enabled his government to
choose substitutes freely, and to make the army mainly an army
of professional soldiers. Nominally, the principle of national
service continued to exist in France, on a scheme under which
five years were spent with the colours and four in the reserve;
but the actual practice was that of a paid regular army, with a
weak and ill-trained militia, and this was the system which
collapsed before the Prussian army in 1870.

The Prussian army of 1870 was a very different force from
that which Frederick William I had raised and drilled, and
Frederick the Great had increased so largely and used so vic-
toriously. The old eighteenth-century army of Prussia had been
broken at Jena by the new instrument which had been forged
in France; and the defeat and *débâcle* had been followed by a
vigorous policy of reform. Two forces concurred to carry this
policy to success. One was the organizing genius of the Prussian
higher command; the other was the emergence, in Germany
at large, and in Prussia even more than elsewhere in Germany,
of a national sentiment provoked by the action of Napoleon.
The military zest and the administrative skill of the Prussian
Government was thus enabled to enlist in its service the spontaneous national ardour of a people already drilled and inured
to war by a century and more of training. Absolutism wedded
itself to nationalism by creating a new national army. Already
in 1807 a Commission of Military Reorganization was formed
under Scharnhorst; and the Commission resolved that the old
army, with its mixture of peasant conscription and foreign
enlistment, should be turned into a national army which was
'the union of all the moral and physical energies of the nation'
Foreign troops were to disappear; in place of a partial conscription of the peasantry, there was to be a general conscription of
the Prussian people with a comparatively short period of service
in the ranks, after which men were to pass into the reserve;
and a new national militia was to form a last line of defence.

The inauguration of the new system was involuntarily provoked by Napoleon himself. He insisted, in 1808, that the Prussian army should be limited to 42,000 men and that Prussia should have no militia. The Prussian command observed the limit; but it passed so many more men through the army, for a shorter period of service, that within a few years the number of those who had been trained to arms was almost four times the amount of the limit. When war came again between Prussia and Napoleon in 1813, a militia or *Landwehr* was also embodied, and another part of the original scheme was thus carried into effect. A new pattern of military organization had been given to the world, which was gradually consolidated in Prussia and ultimately imitated elsewhere. A period of some two or three years of training; the formation of a general reserve from those who had received that training, with the provision of *cadres* and equipment for them in the event of their being called back to the colours—these were the features of the new pattern.[1] It was a system of national service, but it differed from the system which had been enforced in France between 1798 and 1814; on the one hand, it only imposed a short period of active service; on the other hand, it allowed a large expansion in time of emergency. Napoleon had called up only a portion (which it is true grew steadily larger) of those who were liable to serve, but he had called them up for long service; Prussia called up, at any rate in theory, all those who were legally liable to serve, but she only demanded, in the first instance, a period of three years under arms.

The Prussian system, as it stood in 1815, lasted until 1860. It was drastically reinvigorated, but not fundamentally altered, by the reforms of 1860, when the Prussian Regent William, afterwards William I of Prussia, achieved with the aid of Moltke and von Roon one of those military reorganizations which again and again have formed such conspicuous landmarks in

[1] Under the law passed in 1814 there was a universal obligation to serve for three years in the line, two years in the reserve proper, and fourteen years in the *Landwehr*. During the first seven of these fourteen years, members of the *Landwehr* were liable to serve at the front; during the second seven, they were only liable to garrison duty.

the history of Prussian development.[1] The period of service with the colours, which had been allowed to fall to two years, was again to be raised to three; and some forty new regiments were to be created, in order that room might be found in the ranks for the increased population of Prussia (now 18 millions, while fifty years before it had only been 10 millions) and the legal obligation of universal service might thus again become, what for some it had ceased to be, an actual fact. The Prussian Parliament, only recently instituted under the constitution of 1849–50, was opposed to the reorganization, which entailed a heavy permanent expenditure; but by the aid of Bismarck, acting as president of the ministry, the reform was carried in its teeth and made to assume a constitutional as well as a military significance. The victories of Prussia in 1866 and 1870 gave the justification of material success to the new military organization—and also to the constitutional methods by which it had been achieved. Parliament in Prussia had learned its lesson; and another lesson had also been learned by the governments of continental States. The Prussian type of army was the army of victory.[2]

France, as we have seen, had pursued a chequered course in her policy towards conscription during the many vicissitudes of her history between 1789 and 1870. The policy of conscription had been adopted in 1798; it had been renounced at the Restoration; it had been adopted again under the laws of 1832 and 1855; but the permission, and even the encouragement, of the method of 'substitution' had turned into a professional force what professed to be a national army. By 1872

[1] The landmarks in English and French history since 1660 have been revolutions of political sentiment and reforms of political organization—in England the Revolution settlement of 1688 and the Reform Bill of 1832; in France the Revolution of 1789 and the institution of the Third Republic in 1871. The landmarks in Prussian history have been reconstructions of the Prussian army—in the reign of Frederick William I; between 1807 and 1813; and between 1860 and 1864. But these military reconstructions have been accompanied by other and ultimately deeper reforms.

[2] As it stood in 1870, the Prussian system involved $2\frac{1}{2}$ years of service with the colours, 4 in the reserve, and $5\frac{1}{2}$ in the *Landwehr*. The reserve only was intended to supplement the standing army; and the *Landwehr* had its own separate organization. (Sir Frederick Maurice, in the *Camb. Mod. Hist.* xi. 579.)

the Third Republic had already made a final decision in favour of real conscription and a genuine national army. Two causes helped to secure the decision. Not only was the triumph of the Prussian system of conscription an obvious fact; there was also the deeper motive of loyalty to the logic of the Republic. If the Republic rested on the bases of national sovereignty and national self-government, it was the duty of its citizens to secure its existence by national service in its army. A system of universal and personal service was accordingly imposed. Under this system five years were to be spent in full service with the active army, and each citizen was made liable, during the next fifteen years, to recall for temporary service first in the reserve of the active army, and then in the territorial forces and their reserve. The system was more than once varied between 1872 and 1914; but the variations only turned on two points—the total length of service, which by 1914 had risen from twenty to twenty-eight years; and (more especially) the length of service with the active army, which, after having been reduced as low as two, stood in 1914 at three years. In the German army (into which the Prussian army had passed, with the armies of the other German States, under the constitution of 1871) the total period of service, on the eve of the War, was twenty-five years; and only two of these were spent in the active army.[1] The other great States of the Continent—Austria-Hungary, Italy, and Russia—had armies of a similar pattern, based on universal and compulsory service, with a total duration ranging from nineteen to twenty-three years, and a period of training in the active army for either two or three. This was the general system which was plunged into general war in 1914. It is also the general system which, on the whole, has emerged from it, with the one crucial exception that, by Article 173 of the Treaty of Versailles, universal compulsory military service was abolished in Germany, and the German army (limited under Article 160 to a total number of 100,000 'effectives', who must be devoted exclusively to the maintenance of internal order and

[1] It is just to add that the population of the German Empire in 1910 was 65,000,000, and that of France, in 1906, 39,250,000.

the control of frontiers) 'might only be constituted and recruited by means of voluntary enlistment'.

§ 4. *The English Army in the Eighteenth and Nineteenth Centuries*

The English army, it need hardly be said, has pursued an isolated and insular line of development. There was conscription in England during the Civil War in the seventeenth century; and by 1642 both Royalists and Roundheads were forcing into their armies 'mechanics rather than husbandmen, and single men in preference to married', between the ages of 18 and 50. But civil war creates no precedents; and the normal military system of England, since 1660, has known little of conscription. The organization of the English military forces between 1660 and 1815 rested on a distinction between the standing army (which began its life in 1660 with some relics of the previous Cromwellian Army) and the militia. The standing army was a mercenary army raised on a basis of stipendiary contracts made with the king, by a method under which the officers, much as in France, acted as 'middlemen', and made such profits as they could. This standing army, connected by contract with the king, and regarded as a dangerous asset of monarchy, was viewed with a general disfavour; and it was kept under civil control not only by Parliament, which would only pass an annual Act for the maintenance of its discipline, but also by the courts of law, which brought the acts of the soldier, like those of the administrative official, under the cognizance of the common law. The militia had an entirely different position. It did not rest on a basis of contract; it rested on the common-law basis of the obligation of all Englishmen to defend their country against attack. This common-law obligation, interpreted and regulated by Statutes, such as the Militia Acts of 1757 and 1804, involved a form of conscription, with a method of balloting to determine the persons who were actually to serve. Paradoxically, and yet very naturally, this conscript force was the popular part of the English military system. It was no great hardship to be drilled for some summer days in the militia, and it was always permissible to provide substitutes. The local militia was a part and a pillar of local self-government; its control was virtually in the hands of the local gentry; and it could be, and was, regarded as the prop of the Parliamentary State, which was thus able to 'balance' the king's contracted mercenaries by a force sympathetic with the knights of the shire and their brother burgesses.

This eighteenth-century military system, singularly congruous with the general political ideas of the time and the general system of administration,[1] was gradually reformed during the nineteenth century. The reform moved along lines which were generally parallel with the lines followed by the reform of English administration in the same period; but it moved at a slower rate, and it was attended by a more pertinacious survival of elements of the older system. As early as 1783 the Crown began to make its own direct contract with its regular troops; but the old system, under which the officer acted in the capacity of a 'middleman', still continued to exist down to the Crimean War of 1854. The militia survived during the whole of the nineteenth century. It fell into decay after 1815, and the method of balloting was suspended in 1829; it was reorganized on a voluntary basis in 1852, and in 1871 its control was transferred from the lord lieutenants of the counties to the Secretary of State for War. By its side there developed another force, not depending in any way on a common-law obligation, but resting entirely on free consent—the volunteer companies. First created in 1804, under an Act which allowed the Crown to use the services of bodies of volunteers, this force disappeared, except for some cavalry regiments called Yeomanry, after 1815. Re-created in 1859, after the troubled years of the Crimean War and the Indian Mutiny, it became a permanently organized body, with a parliamentary grant for its maintenance; and the English military forces thus consisted at the end of the nineteenth century partly of a 'Regular Army' and partly of 'Auxi-

[1] Just as central administration was weak, so was the central army; just as the 'patented' official was an *entrepreneur* or middleman, so was the commissioned officer; just as Parliament and the judicature regulated the civil State, so they regulated what Blackstone calls the 'military State'; and just as the local gentry controlled local government, so they controlled the local militia.

liary Forces' which included the three several elements of the militia, the yeomanry, and the volunteers.

The reorganization achieved by Haldane in 1907 instituted a new system. Under this system there is henceforth a strengthened Regular Army, consisting not only of the active forces, but also of an army reserve, into which the militia has now been absorbed; and there is also a new Territorial Army, which is formed from the old yeomanry and volunteers (recruited under a new form of enlistment, and for a more effective training), and administered, under the general control of the Secretary of State for War, by County Associations representing the old local principle of the old and vanished militia. This was the system with which England entered the War in 1914, but which was drastically modified during its course by the introduction of conscription. It is the system now in force, with that modification removed.[1]

CHAPTER III
TAXATION

§ 1. *Taxation To-day and in 1660*

FROM one point of view a modern State is a great business undertaking. It is engaged in the supply of services, ranging from those of postmen to that of the King or President; and it will seek to recover the cost of these services from the consumers, who are its own members, on a system partly determined by the amount of their consumption, and partly by their ability to pay—in much the same way as a doctor seeks to recover the cost of his services from his patients. Taxation is thus the reverse side of a great service-rendering organization, and the burden of its incidence will necessarily depend partly on the amount

[1] The English system thus includes two elements. The first is a professional army, composed of troops voluntarily recruited and serving under contract at home and overseas for a period of twelve years (seven, as a rule, in the active army, and five in the reserve) to the number of some 150,000—apart from India. The second is a non-professional force, composed of men (also voluntarily recruited) who continue to pursue their own professions and occupations, but simultaneously receive some military training, and are under a liability in virtue of their terms of enlistment to serve overseas in the event of war if Parliament gives its consent.

of the services supplied, partly on the method by which their
cost is distributed among the different consumers, and partly
on the ability and the economy with which both the supply of
services and the collection of costs are organized. The essential
necessity, upon this basis, is a clear and firm conception of the
State as supplying public services and recovering public costs.
If that conception is clearly held and firmly applied, it will
follow that only public services are met at the public cost. It
will follow, again, that all who benefit by public services must
help to defray public costs, and that no class can escape that
obligation. It will follow, finally, that all who are concerned in
the supply of public services, or the recovery of public costs,
must themselves be public officials and not private 'middlemen'.

Few of these conclusions were drawn in 1660 (or, indeed, for
long afterwards) because the conception of the State on which
they depend had hardly been apprehended. Louis XIV had
indeed attained some idea of the State as incarnate in his own
will and superior to all social interests. But it was only in the
sphere of administration (and even there only partially) that
he succeeded in freeing the action of the State from the play
of Society. In the sphere of taxation he left abundant relics of
the old confusion. It would almost seem as if taxation were
more recalcitrant than other matters of State, and were destined
to remain an exception, and to retain an archaic character, in
an otherwise modernized system. In the first place, the expenses
of the king and his family continued to be confused with those
of the State, and the costs of a great and splendid Royal Household were charged on the general public revenues. This was a
medieval survival, which we may trace in England as well as in
France (the creation of a separate English Civil List, to cover
the separate cost of the Royal Household, belongs to the nineteenth century); but the position was made worse in France
than elsewhere by the fact that the household, which included
a pensioned nobility as well as a splendid court, was a greater
factor in the general economy of the State. In the second place,
there continued to exist a confusion between the management
of State finance and the conduct of a profit-making enterprise.

This confusion showed itself doubly: it appeared in the farming of taxes by contractors, who sought to make private gains from the handling of public revenues; it appeared, again, in the purchase of 'places' by officials, who thus bought for a price what we should now regard as the duty of public service, and then made the exercise of that duty a method of making personal profit. In the third place, and above all, a confusion continued to exist between the system of State-services, with their attendant cost, and the system of social privilege, with its attendant immunities. State-costs, instead of falling on all members of the State with a pressure as uniform as possible, were so distributed as to correspond with a social régime of inequality. The nobility, whether of the sword or the robe, were granted large exemptions, and though it might be pleaded in extenuation that they already served the State with their lives or their labour, and should therefore be excused from the further service of bearing their share of its general costs, the fact remained that the burden of taxation fell peculiarly and predominantly on the poorer classes of the community.

§ 2. *Taxation in France, England, and Prussia during the Eighteenth Century*

Some of these confusions, which were grave defects as well as confusions, may be traced in Europe at large, as well as in France, during the period between 1660 and 1789. But they may be traced particularly in France. Finance was the weakest point in the structure of the *ancien régime*. It may well seem curious that the richest country in Europe should have had the worst financial system—and that in spite of the labours of ministers of finance such as Sully and Colbert; but the answer is perhaps to be found, on the one hand in the court's costly policy of *la gloire*, and, on the other, in a thrifty country's resolve to evade the payment of costs which it had no voice in incurring. These were the fundamental causes of the creation, and perpetuation, of abuses. Direct taxation (the old traditional *taille*, a lump sum for each *élection*, which was then subdivided among *communes*, and finally among the inhabitants of each *commune*; the further *capitation* or poll tax, first instituted in 1695; the still further *vingtième* or percentage on property, first imposed in 1710, and made permanent in 1749) was made to press most on the poorest, just because they had least power of evasion. Indirect taxes, such as excises on alcohol and the *gabelle* or salt tax, fell heavily on the poor by their very nature; and the farming of such taxes, practised because the farmer could turn the screw more effectively under the impulsion of his own interest, added art to nature to increase the burden. Offices were indefinitely multiplied for sale, because office appealed to French instinct, and its sale afforded the one facile source of revenue; but the buyer of office had to recover the cost of his investment, with added interest, and the real burden once more sank down to the bottom of society. 'France would be too rich', wrote a French economist in 1758, 'if the taxes were equitably apportioned.'[1]

They were neither equitably apportioned nor economically collected; nor were they expended, when they reached the hands of the Government, with an equitable regard to the requirements of public service, or on an economical system of public accounts. In the absence of any parliamentary scrutiny, too much was expended with too lavish a hand on the court and on war. In the *anarchie dépensière*[2] of a system of accounts which depended ultimately on the king's will there was no real rigour of audit, and the accounts were invaded not only by peculation, but also by a confusion which made it impossible to ascertain the *état au vrai* of the public finances. Chronic bankruptcy was met by *affaires extraordinaires*, or temporary expedients, which ranged from lotteries and anticipations of revenue to extorted loans and debasement of the coinage. The tax-payer retained, by dint of evasion, some hidden wealth; but he also retained a sense of injustice, provoked not only by unfair distribution and rigorous collection of the taxes, but also by what he could not but regard as selfish and extravagant expenditure. As early as 1707 the great military engineer

[1] Cited in the *Camb. Mod. Hist.*, vol. viii, p. 70.
[2] The phrase is that of Rocquain, *L'Esprit révolutionnaire avant la Révolution*.

Vauban, turning publicist, had urged in his *Dîme royale* the national duty of all to contribute to the cost of public services in proportion to their ability, and he had sketched a new plan of taxation which removed exemptions, imposed on the working classes only $3\frac{1}{2}$ per cent. of the burden of direct taxes, and improved the methods of collection. His book was suppressed, and he died in disgrace in the year of its publication. Absolutism of the French type was too much wedded by its own autocratic nature and by its alliance with social privilege to financial extravagance and injustice; it could not reform them; and in 1789, when it fell, as it were, 'at the point of the purse', it was ruined by them.

The system of the English parliamentary State by its very nature differed fundamentally from that of France. The parliamentary vote of taxes meant parliamentary scrutiny of expenditure. Though the methods of appropriation (which devoted a particular tax to a particular service which it might, or might not, cover) were still imperfect, and though the methods of auditing expenditure, down to 1830, were equally imperfect, owing to the antiquated methods of keeping accounts,[1] there was some genuine public control of the public finances. Farming of the taxes was unknown; and if debt was incurred by the Government it was duly funded, and duly made to bear interest, by the institution of a National Debt, in connexion with the national Bank of England, in 1694. (The word 'national' is significant; the National Debt, as Maitland has noted, 'was owed, not by the Crown, but by "the Publick"'; and the investor in public funds was secured on 'the credit of the Nation'.)[2] Two general defects, however, continued to inhere in the English system during the eighteenth century. In the first place, there was still a confusion between what we may call the account of the king and the general account of the State. On the credit side, the account of the king included not only the

[1] Hatschek remarks (*Englische Verfassungsgeschichte*, p. 715) that though the system of book-keeping by double entry had been known and used in business since the reign of Elizabeth, it was still entirely unknown in the public administration of finances at the end of the eighteenth century.

[2] Introduction to Gierke's *Political Theories of the Middle Age*, p. xxxvi.

revenues of Crown lands, but also the proceeds of the various excises and of the Post Office (which had been instituted by Cromwell's Postage Act of 1657); on the debit side, it was responsible not only for the expenses of the court, but also for much of the expense of administration. It was a step in advance when, in 1760, the Crown received a parliamentary grant of £800,000 a year in lieu of the revenues from Crown lands, the excises, and the Post Office. But if the income of the Crown was placed on a new and better footing, its expenditure had still to be regulated; and a long series of financial reforms (which only began in 1782) had still to be undertaken before the public service of the Crown could be reduced to its proper place in the general system of public services.

The second defect of the English system of public finance in the eighteenth century was graver, and concerned the distribution of the burden of taxes among the different elements of the community. There was no exemption for classes in England; from 1664 onwards, when the clergy surrendered their old right of voting supply separately in convocation, the taxes voted by the national parliament fell on all members of the nation. But it was always possible to lighten the burden of direct taxation, which in the eighteenth century took the form of a land tax, falling mainly on the class of landed gentry who were particularly represented in Parliament; and any reduction of the land tax necessarily entailed an increase in the burden of indirect taxes—the customs levied at the ports and the excises (first introduced by Pym in 1643)[1] on articles of consumption produced within the realm. Here we touch an old issue of politics which is still with us. There is always a natural facility about indirect taxes. The payers of direct taxes, Walpole once remarked, were pigs that squealed if they were touched; the payers of indirect taxes were only sheep that let themselves be sheared in silence. The protectionist system of eighteenth-century England, alleging the need of customs duties for the

---

[1] The history of excise in England is largely a matter of following Dutch example, both in the seventeenth century, and afterwards in the eighteenth, when Adam Smith drew attention to Dutch methods.

support of English agriculture and industry, lent the sanction
of high policy to justify a natural facility and a natural pull of
interests. In the time of Walpole direct taxes varied in yield from
£1,250,000 to £2,150,000: indirect taxes remained fairly steady
at about £4,300,000—about double the amount of direct taxes
even when they stood at their highest. The balance of English
taxation was tilted, and it was only at the end of the eighteenth
century, with the reforms of Pitt, that it began to be redressed.

The Prussian system of taxation in the period between 1660
and 1789 was superficially similar to that of France, but fundamentally different. Like the king of France, the Prussian King
was an absolute ruler, who imposed his taxes to suit a military
policy. He had his *Steuerräthe*, analogous to the French *intendants*, for the local supervision of taxes and finance. Under
Frederick the Great, as we have seen, the Prussian customs and
excise were organized on the French model, and largely managed
by French officials. But these analogies and connexions lay
on the surface; and there was a fundamental difference in the
peculiar genius of Prussian absolutism, which sacrificed the
revenues of the Crown to the requirements of the State, and
practised a severe economy both at the court and in the cost of
public administration. Frederick William I, by a prudent hus-
bandry, made his Crown lands yield almost one-half of his
whole revenue. If he excused his nobles (except in east Prussia)
from taxation, he imposed on them a severe burden of military
duty; and while he made the towns and the peasantry bear the
burden of taxes—largely in the shape of the urban excise and
the monopoly of salt which had been introduced by the Great
Elector—he also made his *Steuerräthe* promote the prosperity of
his towns and the development of Prussian industries. He
accumulated a great army, but he also accumulated a large
balance; and he left, at the end of his reign, a war treasure of
6 million thalers, which was equivalent to nearly one and a half
years of the whole revenue which he derived from Crown lands
and from taxes.

Frederick the Great was no less prudent than his father, and
in spite of his many wars he left a treasure of 50 million thalers,

amounting to more than two and a quarter years of a revenue which was itself triple the amount that his father had collected. But Prussia suffered heavily under the strain imposed by a policy so rigorous. The coinage was debased; the monopoly of salt became a salt conscription, under which every family was compelled to purchase a quota; monopolies of tobacco and coffee were added to that of salt; excises (administered by his French superintendent) were imposed on all kinds of meat except pork, as well as on beer and spirits. It is true that Frederick, in a spirit of paternal protectionism, strove hard to promote the industries of Prussia—iron and timber,[1] linen and silk and velvet—and it has been calculated that in the latter half of his reign he spent 60 million thalers on economic development. But it is also true that the Crown lands were heavily rack-rented, that every consumer was heavily mulcted, and that the peasants were only allowed to spend on themselves a little more than a third of the money they earned.[2] The death of Frederick in 1783 was immediately followed by the abolition of the monopolies of coffee and tobacco, the dismissal of the French staff in the excise, and the beginning of a more generous policy in regard to Crown rents. Prussia remained solvent, though by 1790 the war treasure had already disappeared; and the excellence of her administrators, coupled with the growth of her territory and its progressive economic development, continued to ensure her solvency.

§ 3. *The Development of Taxation in the Three Countries since 1800*

In the history of taxation, as in that of administration and conscription, a new epoch begins in western Europe with the beginning of the nineteenth century. It would be impossible to recount the developments of that epoch; it is only possible

---

[1] He even issued instructions to housemaids about the use of touch-wood, instead of rags, as tinder to light a fire. This attention to detail may remind us of Napoleon, regulating the theatres of Paris during his Moscow campaign, or of the medieval Emperor Frederick II, determining by an imperial mandate what the maids of his palace should wear.

[2] In France, on Taine's calculation, the peasant had only one-fifth (19 francs in every 100 francs of net income).

to suggest some few of its salient features. In the first place, taxation begins to be adjusted to the cost of the public services which are genuinely required by the national State, and to be imposed without respect of persons on all who share in those services. The old confusions, by which expenses of State were mixed with the expenses of Court, and social privilege was allowed to distort the incidence of State taxes, now disappeared; and just as the conception of the national State altered administration and transformed the army, so it altered and transformed the system of public finances. In the second place, the growth of national parliaments, on the English model, supplied an instrument both for determining the necessary services and their respective costs, and for settling the methods by which those costs should be met. Absolutism—except in Prussia, and only there at a heavy cost—had failed to discharge that function; it had not succeeded either in settling the relative claims of the different services, or in apportioning on any basis of general satisfaction the incidence of the taxes which they involved; its great defect, and its final nemesis, had been finance. In the new system, as it is already enunciated in the Declaration of Rights of 1789, 'all citizens have the right to settle, by themselves or their representatives, the necessity of making a public contribution, and to give their free consent thereto'. In the third place the battle is still engaged, if it is fought on the new basis of the national State, between the claims of indirect taxation and those of direct. Two factors affect the fortunes of the battle. One is the growth, among the European nations, of democratic and equalitarian sentiment, tending in favour of a system of direct taxation which will fall most heavily on those who are best able to pay their contribution. The other is the growth of national protectionism, which seeks at once to promote economic prosperity and to accumulate a revenue by a system of indirect taxes imposed upon foreign imports. It is a system which, from one point of view, seems to kill two birds with one stone; it is a system which, from another, seems to make each nation derive its revenue from taxes on other nations; but from both points of view it has exerted, and continues to exert, a large attraction. It was not new in itself; it had been practised by Colbert, and it had been practised industriously by Frederick the Great. It was only new in its application to the national State, in a new economic era of rapid development and growing international commerce.

In France the first effect of the Revolution, following the logic of its principles, had been to reduce indirect taxes to a minimum, and to make taxation predominantly direct. This was in accordance with the Declaration of Rights of 1789, which had stated that 'for the maintenance of the public forces, and the expenses of the administration, a common contribution is indispensable, and this contribution must be equally divided among all the citizens in proportion to their means'. Napoleon, fortunate in the possession of 'extraordinary external receipts' (a designation which covered indemnities and requisitions), made little change in the direct taxes, but he gradually introduced a heavy burden of indirect taxation. Internally, *octrois* and excises—the *droits réunis* which France came to hate as she hated conscription—were again imposed. There were taxes on liquors; there was a salt tax, imposed in 1805; there was a tobacco monopoly, instituted in 1810. Externally, and at the ports, tariffs were regular after 1802; and the detailed tariff of 1806 was the basis of French tariffs for most of the nineteenth century. The system of *anesthésie fiscale*,[1] in which indirect taxes are predominant, was adopted in 1815, and continued long afterwards. Perhaps it suited the genius of France, which preferred to pay its taxes through monopolies and similar indirect methods, or at official moments of 'registration' and by way of the purchase of stamps; and yet the genius of France was in this respect not peculiar to France. In any case it was not until the beginning of the twentieth century that a searching and scientific system of direct taxation was attempted. What had delayed its development was partly an inherited prejudice against the extension of direct taxes, which were associated (in spite of the Declaration of 1789) with the oppression of the old régime, and partly, again, an inherited tradition of indirect

[1] Barthélemy, *Le Gouvernement de la France*, c. xi, sect. ii, *ad initium*.

taxation, which had been reaffirmed by the tariff policy of 1806 and afterwards; but it was also a rigid interpretation of the principle of equality, which was held to exclude the application of the principle of progression to direct taxes, on the ground that any surcharging of great fortunes and large incomes involved inequality of incidence. But the cause of equity was pleaded against that of mere equality; it was argued that equality itself —if not as between individual payers of direct taxes, at any rate as between the payers of direct taxes in general and the general body of payers of indirect taxes—involved the system of progressive direct taxation; by a law of 1901 the principle was applied to the inheritance of fortunes, and by another law of 1914 to general income. The old system of *réalité de l'impôt*, under which taxation fell on things, and was therefore indirect, begins to yield to a new system in which taxation falls primarily on *personalité économique.*[1]

There was no revolutionary change in the history of English taxation at the end of the eighteenth century. But if there was no revolution, there was a movement of financial, or as it was called by Burke 'economical', reform; and we may date the beginnings of that movement in 1782, exactly half a century before the political reform of 1832. The first effort of financial reform turned on the royal expenditure. In 1782, under the influence and guidance of Burke, the expenses chargeable against the King's account began to be brought into order, and henceforth, by a steady process, they were gradually confined to the actual expenses of the King's Household. The change which had begun in 1760, when the King's income had been made a fixed sum derived from parliamentary grant, was thus carried to its logical conclusion, and made to include the regulation of his expenditure as well as his income. A clear distinction was drawn between the personal account of the King and the general account of the State; and by the accession of Queen Victoria in 1837 this distinction assumed its modern form, in which the income of the monarchy (save for the revenues of the Duchy of Lancaster) is derived from a parliamentary grant

[1] Idem, c. xi, sect. ii, *ad finem.*

made for the purpose, and its expenditure (save for an exiguous pension list) is confined to the service of the household.

The regulation of the King's income and expenditure in a separate account not only removed an old source of confusion; it also secured the necessary basis on which Parliament could proceed to regulate the national accounts, and to improve its own imperfect methods of appropriation of supply to services and of audit of annual expenditure. This is the second effort of financial reform; and it began during the long ministry of the younger Pitt (1783–1801), which in so many ways formed an epoch in the history of English public finance. One of Pitt's great achievements was the institution in 1787 of a single Consolidated Fund into which the whole yield of customs and excises was to be paid, and he thus laid the basis for a system of deliberate appropriations from a single general fund in lieu of the old method of haphazard appropriations from a number of particular funds. The problem of a genuine audit of expenditure still remained to be solved; and its solution was not attained until the reign of William IV and the first half of the reign of Queen Victoria. A condition of any solution was the adoption of a proper method of book-keeping, and such a method was provided, soon after 1830, by what a German scholar[1] has called 'the Reception of the French Budget-system'. This meant a system of national book-keeping by double entry, in place of the old method of a number of unconnected accounts; and on this basis it now became possible both for the Chancellor of the Exchequer to 'open' a true budget for the ensuing year, and for the Comptroller and Auditor-General (an officer first instituted in 1834, but only attaining his final position in 1866) to make a true survey of past expenditure in his annual audit. Parliamentary control of public finances, which had existed in principle ever since 1660, or at any rate since 1688, was thus at last made effective.

[1] Hatschek, *Englische Verfassungsgeschichte*, pp. 718–21. He assigns to Bowring, the biographer of Bentham, the credit of having studied the French methods of keeping public accounts, and of having introduced into England, on the French model, the system of national book-keeping by double entry, which had been practised in France since the eighteenth century.

There were technical matters; but the serious and practical problem was that of reforming both direct and indirect taxes, and of determining their relative incidence. The reform of direct taxation began when Pitt in 1798 relegated the old land tax to the position of a perpetual charge on land, and instituted in 1799 a new income tax. The income tax was regarded as a war measure; it was dropped as such in 1815; and its subsequent history was to turn on the policy of England in regard to protection and customs duties. Here, too, a policy of reform had already been begun by Pitt, but his work, interrupted by war in 1792, tended rather to simplify collection than to make any fundamental change in incidence. A more drastic reform began about 1825; it received a great impetus when in 1842 and 1845 Peel abolished a great number of duties, and in 1846 removed the duty on corn; it was concluded by the budgets of Gladstone and more especially the budget of 1860. England embarked on a policy of free trade in lieu of national protectionism; and she paid the price for the abolition of protective customs (the more readily as she profited industrially by the change of policy) in the shape of a revived income tax, which since 1842 has been a permanent part of our financial system. But the policy of free trade still left a number of lucrative customs duties, imposed solely for the sake of revenues, and falling mainly on tobacco, tea, and alcohol; and it also left a large revenue from excises levied on corresponding articles. In the beginning of the twentieth century customs and excises still produced about £60 millions, while the yield of income tax, levied at an average rate of one shilling in the pound, was about £40 millions.

An important change had, however, begun in 1894, and it had begun in the sphere of estate duties. Technically such duties belong, from one point of view, to the category of indirect taxation; like customs and excise, they are imposed upon objects at the time of transference of possession. Practically, however, they may be said to be imposed, like direct taxes, on the *personalité économique* in which possession is vested.[1] The

---

[1] They differ, however, from other charges on *personalité économique* in being levied not on income, but on capital.

change of 1894, which increased the rate of these duties and applied to them the principle of progression, according to the amount transferred, introduced a new phase of taxation. The same method of increase of rate and application of the principle of graduation has now been extended to income tax; and by 1930, out of a total yield from taxes of £685 millions, income tax (with the surtax on large incomes) produced nearly £300 millions while customs and excise together produced about £250 millions, and duties on estates yielded some £80 millions of the remainder. The revolution is obvious. Some would describe it as the triumph of a socialist policy of the conscription of wealth. More justly it may be described as the result of the conjunction of two causes—an increasing growth of State services, and an increasing application, for the purpose of meeting the costs of those services, of the old liberal principle of equality, interpreted in a larger sense. But it must be admitted that the new interpretation has carried us a long way. Not only has it been decided that there must be more equality in practice between direct and indirect taxation, and that, in order to achieve this result, the principle of progression should be applied to direct taxation, but a new idea has also been suggested, that the instrument of taxation, instead of being used simply and solely to cover the cost of State services, should also be used to redistribute property and income. This would make equality not only the method, but also the object, of the imposition of taxes. The idea is as old as Bentham, but it is an idea which would transform taxation (in its etymology and its past history an 'assessment of costs' between parties) into something new.

The history of taxation in Prussia since the end of the eighteenth century is complicated by her growing connexion with the rest of Germany. Solvent in 1790, Prussia emerged from the Napoleonic wars with a debt of over 200 million thalers and an annual deficit of 2 millions. Relief was found by the abolition of internal customs and the introduction in 1818 of a system of free trade between the different Prussian territories. This system made Prussia prosperous internally; it was accompanied by the imposition of moderate duties on foreign manufactures;

and it brought relief. Eventually the other German States were induced to join the Prussian system of internal free trade and external tariffs, and by a series of treaties, beginning in 1819, a *Zollverein* was gradually spread over Germany. This economic unity was the preparation, and in no small measure the cause, of the political unity which Germany achieved in 1871. Under these conditions it was the area of indirect taxes which, owing to its connexion with political developments, assumed a growing importance. In the German Empire, down to 1914, the imperial or federal expenditure was met from the yield of customs and certain of the excises (which produced the greater part of the federal income), by the profits of the postal system and the railways, and by federal contributions from the different States. Prussia, like the other States of the Empire, had her own financial system, with a revenue greater by far than that of the Empire. The results of the war, and the working of the new constitution of 1919, have made fundamental changes. Prussia in 1930 had a budget of only 4,000 million marks, to the 11,000 millions of the *Reich* (of which, however, 3,500 millions were paid over to States and local bodies); and the vast new expenditure of the *Reich* had entailed a new distribution of taxes in which the yield from customs was only about one-tenth of the whole.

CHAPTER IV

SOCIAL SERVICES

§ 1. *Church and State in the Sphere of Social Services*

THE weight of taxation at the present time is principally due to the cost of the old services of the State, and more particularly of the military service. The cost of liquidating the wars of the past and of preparing new defences against the wars of the future is more than one-half of the total cost of State management in Great Britain to-day.[1] But a new burden has been

---

[1] The cost is mainly that of liquidation, or in other words, the payment of interest on the National Debt. The current expenditure on military services is only a quarter of the total expenditure on supply services.

added to the Exchequer of the modern State by its assumption of services which, at any rate in their modern dimensions, may fairly be regarded as new. We may call these services by the generic name of 'social'. They include, in the broader sense of that word, the service of education as well as 'social services' proper. They are the services by which the State secures to its members the enjoyment of two rights, each of which has received a progressive interpretation, and, with it, an extended guarantee—the physical right to life, health, and a proper standard of subsistence; and the mental and moral right to development of intelligence and character.[1]

In the system of medieval thought it was regarded as the duty and service of the Church both to assist the indigent, as a necessary work of Christian charity, and to provide some scheme of education, as a necessary exercise of that power of teaching which (along with the power of celebrating the sacraments and the power of exercising jurisdiction) was inherent in the ecclesiastical hierarchy.[2] The transference of these duties or services from the Church to the State is a long and gradual process. Three things may be said of that process. In the first place, the activity of the State was generally an improvement on that of the Church—not because it was in its nature higher than the Church, but because its administrative power, bearing directly on all its members, gave it larger resources than those of the Church, which had only been able to deal with the problem of pauperism in terms of a charity that was naturally haphazard, just as it had only been able to deal with the problem of education in terms of religious teaching that naturally tended to be mainly confined to the recruitment of the clergy.[3]

[1] 'The purpose of the public elementary school is to form and strengthen the character, and to develop the intelligence, of the children entrusted to it.' (Introduction to the Code for English public elementary schools, as issued by the Board of Education from 1904 to 1926.)

[2] The power of the hierarchy is sometimes regarded as a triple power, including (first and foremost) a *potestas ordinis* in matters concerning the Sacraments, a *potestas jurisdictionis*, and a *potestas docendi*. But the *potestas docendi* is usually subsumed under the *potestas jurisdictionis*, and education is thus regarded as a part of discipline.

[3] On the other hand, this increased activity of the State has not rendered the activity of the Church otiose. The extension of the political sphere still leaves intact

In the second place, the process was more rapid in Protestant countries than in Catholic—not, again, because the former had a genius superior to that of the latter, but because the secularization of religious endowments which accompanied the Reformation so much diminished the resources of the Church that Protestant States were necessarily compelled to assume some of its old functions. In the third place, the State was compelled in all countries alike to guarantee physical rights to its members (on a very modest scale, it is true) long before it began to recognize their mental and moral rights. In England, for example, there was something of a State system for dealing with the problem of pauperism by the beginning of the reign of Elizabeth: there was no State system of education until the middle of the reign of Queen Victoria.

§ 2. *The Three Periods in the History of State Social Services*

There are three periods in the history of the dealings of the modern State in western Europe with the problem of the rights of its members to life, health, and a proper standard of subsistence. The first is the period before the Industrial Revolution. This is a period which, in England, comes to an end about 1760; but on the Continent, where the Revolution was later in making itself felt, it lasts till the middle of the nineteenth century.[1] During this period the State is mainly concerned with the problems of a rural population, and it has to 'relieve' (at the same time as it taxes) a peasantry scattered all over its territories. The second period, comparatively brief on the Continent, but more prolonged in England, is that which lies

a social sphere of voluntary activity; and the Church is the greatest agent in this sphere. Nor must we forget that Christian charity, however imperfect it may be in its results, has this advantage over public assistance in the scale of moral values, that it is a spontaneous moral activity proceeding from a moral motive, and not the automatic performance of a legal duty.

[1] The cotton industry in France, which was the first to be revolutionized, was becoming a factory industry in the latter part of the reign of Louis Philippe (*c.* 1840); but the other textile trades had not at that date adopted the power-loom. Germany at that time was still largely in the stage of 'domestic' industry; and 'the German iron industry was still a half-rural, a woodland, trade' (Professor Clapham, *Camb. Mod. Hist.*, vol. x, pp. 753-7).

between the beginning of the Industrial Revolution and the consolidation of unions of organized workers and employers with which the State has now to reckon, and which it must take into partnership in dealing with social problems. In this period the State is concerned with a mass of uprooted country-workers employed in the factories of the towns or in mining centres, and it deals with them as best it can by Factory Acts, Truck Acts, Mines Regulation Acts, and the like. England developed a system of control which we may call by the general name of Factory Legislation in the years between the first Factory Act of 1802 and the consolidating Act of 1901, which forms a general code for all factories and workshops; and as the Industrial Revolution spread from England to the Continent, this code spread with it to France and Germany and other countries. It is difficult to date the beginning of the third period, but it may be assigned roughly to the year 1880. It is true that the period of factory legislation extends beyond 1880, and, indeed, is still with us; it is also true that even before 1880, in countries in which trade unions had grown and acquired some freedom of action, they had already become informal co-operators and virtual partners with the State, in the sense that they were already using their collective strength to bargain for standards of health and subsistence at the same time that the State was also enforcing similar standards by legislation. But we may date a new epoch, none the less, from the year 1880. In England, by the Acts of 1871 and 1875, trade unions had now acquired a new measure of freedom; their process of collective bargaining for standards was recognized by the law of the land; a 'new unionism' was beginning, and on its basis representatives of the unions were soon to enter Parliament, and to link the factor of collective bargaining outside to the factor of legislative enactment of standards within. Germany followed a somewhat different line; but Bismarck's legislation in the decade following 1880, which enlisted employers and workers to co-operate with the State in schemes of social insurance for the maintenance of standards of health and subsistence, forms a landmark not only in the history of Germany, but also in that of western Europe.

If English factory legislation had spread to Germany, German social insurance was to spread in the twentieth century to England.

§ 3. *The Agrarian Period and Poor Relief*

In the agrarian period prior to the rise of industrialism, France, England, and Prussia were all concerned with the problem of rural indigence, and their governments were content to guarantee the elementary right to life by rescuing the poor from absolute starvation. The most developed system formed for this purpose was that which was created in England by the Tudor kings and Parliaments between 1536 and 1601. In its original intention the Tudor system of poor relief was designed to provide work (and even housing) as well as mere relief; and it was meant to be administered by each parish, which was to raise and apply a fund for these several purposes. In its actual execution it fell into the hands of the local gentry of each shire, and it was administered by them on the basis of mere relief—relief which by 1795 had come to assume the form of allowances paid from the parish rates in aid of farm wages. Condemned, and not unjustly, as a method of pauperization which only depressed the rate of wages, this system was superseded, under the Poor Law Amendment Act of 1834, by a new system which entailed both a political and an economic revolution. Politically, the revolution was twofold; not only were the justices of the peace dethroned in favour of elected boards administering relief in 'unions' or groups of parishes, but a new central administrative authority was created to supervise the activity of these boards. Economically, the principle of indoor relief, to be given only in workhouses built for the purpose by each union, was enunciated; the old method of outdoor relief in aid of wages was to be abolished, and wages were thus to be left free to find a higher level. But the principle enunciated could not be maintained in practice, and outdoor relief continued to be given, both to the aged and to the unemployed. Two modifications have been made in our own days in this system, which we inherited from our agrarian past, but carried, in the modified form of 1834, into our industrial present. On the one hand, the adoption of the German scheme of 'social insurance', side by side with the old English scheme of 'poor relief', has introduced not only a new factor, but also a new complication. On the other hand, by a political change, the administration of poor relief, now termed public assistance, has been transferred, under an Act of 1929, to the county councils (and the councils of county boroughs), acting for the purpose through a special public assistance committee.[1]

The methods of relief in France and Prussia followed different lines. In Prussia, during the eighteenth century, the Kings were the agents of an informal system of poor relief. They pursued a policy of encouraging aided immigration into their dominions, which formed a sort of colonial land for new settlers; and this policy, if it served their own purposes, also helped to meet the problem of German poverty and to multiply small rural holdings. They also instituted corn depots, and they were able by this means to stabilize prices and to keep the cost of living comparatively steady. The same general method of absolutism was also pursued, along somewhat different lines, in eighteenth-century France. There was, indeed, one great difference: the French King could still count, down to 1789, on the co-operation of a wealthy Catholic Church, which maintained hospitals, centres of outdoor relief, and other charitable foundations. But the Crown was also forced to come to the rescue: there was a distribution of the *pain du roi* at the Louvre, for which the beggars and vagabonds of Paris fought; and the King's Council allotted to each *intendant* a share of the royal bounty, which he proceeded to distribute among the *communes*, superintending them closely in their administration of their share.

---

[1] It is interesting to notice the close connexion between the history of the English poor law and the history of the development of English local government. Poor relief was the ground of the development of the parish as an organ of local government in the sixteenth century; poor relief was the area in which the justices established themselves as the local governing authority after 1700; and it was in the sphere of poor relief that, in 1834, a new régime (of elected local bodies, and of central administrative supervision of these bodies) first appeared.

The immediate effect of the Revolution in France was to destroy both the old charitable foundations of the Church and the royal bounty. A heavy burden was thus thrown on the local authorities, more especially in the towns (the peasantry of the country had profited by the Revolution, both in escaping old burdens and in acquiring new land), and Napoleon did something to enable them to meet the burden. The *octrois* imposed in towns were specially devoted to charity, along with a part of the proceeds of municipal property; the prefects and mayors were active in relief; and the many public works undertaken by Napoleon's government provided a new source of employment. But France, in her normal condition since 1815 a great self-sufficing country, with an industrious peasant population, has not been afflicted by the problems of England, and the English reforms of 1834 had no parallel in contemporary French legislation. A law of the Third Republic, passed in 1871, allowed each department to initiate methods of general assistance, and compelled all to assist lunatics, destitute children, and those who from sickness or old age were unable to work. But no separate organization was created, exclusively devoted to the relief of pauperism. The departments and the communes administered asylums, institutions for destitute children, and hospitals as part of their general duties; and in the sphere of 'general assistance' relief was given by *bureaux de bienfaisance* from funds which, if they were partly derived from communal contributions, were also derived from endowments and from charitable gifts. On the one hand, France linked poor relief with general local government; on the other, she linked voluntary to public contribution. The Prussian system, as it developed during the nineteenth century, was equally unlike the English. Poor relief was one of the functions of the new system of local government which, as we have seen, was elaborated in Prussia from the days of Stein onwards. In the towns it was administered by a special committee, containing co-opted members (or 'selected citizens') in addition to aldermen and councillors, and acting under the presidency of a professional burgomaster; special poor rates were not levied;

and a system of unpaid visitors, on the model of Elberfeld, was common. In the rural communes poor relief was similarly one of the functions of the ordinary activity of local government.

§ 4. *The First Industrial Period and Factory Legislation*

These systems of poor relief were the first form of social service performed by the State. Beginning in the first of the three periods which we have distinguished, they have continued to exist, with changes in scope and methods of administration, in the later periods. But new forms of service to meet new conditions have also been added, and the addition has been accompanied by a change of general ideas. The old idea which underlay the early forms of poor relief (as it also underlay the early beginnings of popular education in England) was that of a concession made *ex gratia* to the indigent members of a class called the 'labouring poor'; the new idea, which gradually takes its place, is that of a right guaranteed *ex jure* to the member of a civic community by the simple title of his membership. But the new idea was slow in developing, and the old notions —notions, as we may call them, of 'the philanthropic boon'— still permeated the beginnings of the new social services which a new industrial age demanded.

The first phase of these new services—the phase which appears in the whole system of factory legislation—may best be illustrated from England, where its history covers the whole of the nineteenth century. The new social problem was the factory, and beyond the factory the factory-town. Men began to recognize that there was such a thing as a right to health, over and above the right to mere life which the old system of poor relief had recognized; and they drew the conclusion that, in order to guarantee this right, the State must perform the service of providing some decent minimum of general sanitation in the town, and of securing—in the factory, the mining centre, and the industrial aggregation of every kind—the hours and the general conditions of labour which were necessary to the health and the physical well-being of the worker. The movement of this legislation began in a moral spirit of philanthropic indignation; it ended in a civic consciousness of the duty of providing a civic service. It involved the State in an interference with the contract of employment, or rather in a regulation of the basic terms on which that contract was to be made; it involved it in a system of inspection to ensure that the basic terms were faithfully observed. The first Factory Act of 1802 was followed by many successors, especially the Act of 1833, which introduced factory inspectors, and the 'Ten Hours Bill' of 1847; and the whole series of Factory Acts was eventually codified in 1901. What had been done for factories was extended to mining centres by the Mines Regulation Act of 1842 and a succession of later Acts; it was extended to transport workers by the Merchant Shipping Act of 1876 and the Regulation of Railways Act of 1889; it was extended, finally, by various Workshop and Shop Hours Acts to nearly the whole of production and exchange. Beyond the service thus rendered to the various classes of workers in their various occupations, the State undertook another service when, in 1848, by the Public Health Act, it began to guarantee to all its members the necessary conditions of general health. It began to insist that houses as well as workshops, and the conditions of living as well as of working, should satisfy what has been termed 'a national minimum of sanitation': it began to provide, in the largest sense of the words, a 'public medical service' which would make its insistence effective.

§ 5. *The Second Industrial Period and the System of Social Insurance*

The new period which begins about 1880 continues, but also transcends, the principle of a social service directed to securing the health of the working classes and the general community. It continues and it extends that principle, when by the Housing of the Working Classes Act of 1903 (already preceded by the Artisans' Dwelling Act of 1874), and still more by the successive Housing Acts of recent years, it passes beyond its original purpose of securing a minimum standard of sanitation in existing dwelling-houses, and begins to organize and to aid the provision of new housing on a large scale. More important, however, is the growing adoption of a new principle that it is the function of the State to co-operate in securing a proper standard of subsistence. This may seem, at first sight, nothing more than a new form of the old service of poor relief; but it is something fundamentally different in more than one respect. Poor relief is only concerned with the pauper: the new service deals with the general body of workers. Poor relief is a recognition of the bare right to life, and a rescue from utter starvation (though the action of English justices of the peace made it temporarily something more at the end of the eighteenth and the beginning of the nineteenth century): the new service is a recognition of the right to live on a decent standard of subsistence, and a guarantee of that standard against the menace of sickness, unemployment, and old age. Above all, poor relief is a service which leaves the pauper passive; the new service is one which, in various ways, enlists the body of workers, and also of their employers, in active co-operation with the State, on the basis of a joint contribution made by all the parties.

If the characteristic of the first of our three periods is 'poor relief', and that of the second 'factory legislation', the characteristic of this third and last period is 'social insurance'. The new system began in Germany with the successive laws which Bismarck carried in 1883, 1884, and 1889, with the object of defeating the Socialists by making the State itself socialist. The law of 1883 insured workmen against sickness; they were themselves to pay two-thirds of the cost and their employers the other third; the payments were to be collected and the benefits paid by approved societies, which might be connected with factories or trade unions as well as with local communes or voluntary clubs. The law of 1884 insured workmen against the risk of accident, at the cost of their employers, who formed themselves into industrial associations for mutual protection in meeting the new liability. The law of 1889 insured workmen against invalidity and old age; they were to contribute equally with their employers, but the State was also to contribute to the pension ultimately paid to the disabled or superannuated worker; and the State was thus linked in finance, as well as in general regulation, with the organization of the world of industry.

The German scheme spread to England and France in the beginning of the twentieth century. In England the Workmen's Compensation Act of 1897 'introduced into the law', as Dicey has said, 'the new principle that an employer must . . . insure his workmen against the risks of their employment'. In 1908 the Old Age Pensions Act introduced a system of pensions, entirely paid by the State, for all persons over the age of 70 whose means were not sufficient for their support. (This system was different from the German scheme of 1889, which only dealt with workers superannuated from unemployment, and dealt with them on a basis of contributory insurance; but a new German law of 1911, while still maintaining the basis of insurance, instituted a new scheme of old age pensions for workers generally on their attaining the age of 65.) In 1909, going beyond the German model of social insurance, and adopting a new method of guaranteeing a decent minimum of subsistence, the English Parliament passed a Trade Boards Act which secured a minimum wage, enforced by the State, to workers in those sweated industries in which there were no trade unions adequate to the function of collective bargaining. In 1911, once more on the German model, the National Insurance Act introduced a scheme of health insurance in which employers, workers, and the State were all to co-operate and to contribute; but the Act went beyond its model in also introducing a scheme of unemployment insurance on the same tripartite basis for a number of specified industries. An Unemployed Workmen Act of 1905 had already begun to apply methods other than those of poor relief to the problem of unemployment; but it was a new and important step when the method of joint social insurance against unemployment was applied, by the Act of 1911, to industries such as iron-founding, ship-building, and mechanical engineering.

The development in France was less rapid and varied. An Act of 1905 provided for the relief of the aged poor (on attaining the age of 70), and of infirm or permanently incurable persons, from funds supplied by the State and by the departments and communes. In the same year France began to imitate the Ghent system (first instituted in 1901) by which public funds are used to supplement in a fixed proportion the benefits paid by trade unions to their unemployed members. In 1910 the French Parliament passed an Old Age Pensions Act, providing pensions for wage-earners from a fund contributed by employers and workers and supplemented by the State. In 1913, by a policy peculiar to France, but dictated by the prevalence of infant mortality and the fear of a stationary population, an act was passed for giving aid to large families for each child beyond the third.

The advance of the present century, which was already marked before the War, has been equally marked in the years since 1918. The States of western Europe had called upon their citizens to serve them in war as they had never done before, and they were impelled in turn by a natural logic to provide services for their citizens in peace on a new and larger scale. In England, in 1918, the scope of trade boards was extended, until they embraced some forty industries and a million and a half employees; and the trade boards began to fix standard, or regular, wages instead of a minimum rate below which wages must not fall. The Widows, Orphans, and Old Age Contributory Pensions Act of 1925 added a new scheme of social insurance to the previous grant of free State pensions in 1908; the scope of unemployment insurance was extended until it covered most of the persons who came within the scope of health insurance (about 14 millions in all); and new responsibilities for housing were undertaken by the State under a succession of Housing Acts. It has been calculated that, while £22,600,000 was spent on social services in 1891, £338,500,000[1] was being expended in 1925; and the expenditure has risen since. France,

---

[1] Of this amount war pensions accounted for £66,500,000 and education for nearly £90,000,000. Insurance (both health and unemployment) and old age pensions cost £109,000,000; Poor Relief a little over £40,000,000; and the remaining £33,000,000 was spent mainly on housing (£18,400,000), and on public health and the care of lunatics and mental deficients.

after long discussion, passed in 1928 a general law for compulsory social insurance covering sickness, maternity, and invalidity as well as old age. The new Germany created by the Constitution of Weimar also travelled far in the decade between 1920 and 1930. Not only did it adopt a system which involved the State in fixing wages on a large scale, as the authority of final resort after arbitration had been attempted; not only did it institute unemployment insurance, and extend the general principle of social insurance to clerical workers: it also recast (in 1924) the old system of poor relief and placed it on the new basis of a general *Fürsorge*[1] which comprehended in its scope the derelicts of the War and the *rentiers* who found their insurance benefits or other *rentes* inadequate. In addition it instituted, by a law of 1922, a system of public *Jugendhilfe* which provided for the young not only education, but also, where it was needed, a semi-parental care, exercised through *Jugendämter*, along with a training in general fitness (both of body and of mind) for proper membership of society.

A word which became current in Germany during this period was the word *Wohlfahrt*; and we in England have also begun to talk of 'welfare work' in our factories, and have instituted, under the Mining Industry Act of 1920, a Miners' Welfare Fund. Perhaps the word holds a key to the future; and the State, which has risen from poor relief to factory legislation, and from factory legislation to social insurance, may rise to some new service of public welfare. But the State is not all; and we have to reflect that voluntary social self-help, which has always gone hand in hand with the State, has its own sphere of activity, and may even be the better organ for much of the service of welfare.[2] If we make the State a Pandora, the source of 'all gifts', we may be surprised at some of the results which emerge from Pandora's box.

We may compare our own change from 'poor relief' to 'public assistance'; but the *Reichsfursorge* of Germany went farther than our public assistance.

On the new municipal housing estates in England, for example, voluntary 'community associations' are being formed, and are seeking in various ways (by the provision of community centres and the development of community activities) to discharge a service of welfare for the benefit of their members.

CHAPTER V

EDUCATION

§ 1. *The Development of State Education in France*

THE connexion between religion and education, interpreted to mean that it was the function of the Church and its clergy to provide a system of general instruction, was long an accepted principle in western Europe, both in Catholic and in Protestant countries. By Catholics 'the power of teaching' was regarded as one of the powers inherent in the Church; and in Catholic countries the actual work of instruction fell to the religious orders, particularly to the great order of the Jesuits, down to the middle of the eighteenth century, when the Age of Enlightenment, stimulated by the troubles which beset the Jesuit Order, began to turn to the idea of State education. Nor were the Protestant Reformers favourable to the principle of a system of national education conducted by the State: they were rather concerned with the production of an educated clergy and the dissemination of religious knowledge by its means. If Scotland, in the seventeenth century, instituted parochial schools, they were intended to be administered under the direct supervision of the Kirk; and the Scottish system of bursaries, which opened a wide door to the universities, was largely designed for the better recruitment of the clergy. Protestant England followed a different line of development; but it was religious considerations which mainly determined that line. If a system of national education was delayed until 1870, it was not the backwardness of the country, or its blindness to the need of education, which was responsible; it was rather that the long rivalry of Anglican and Nonconformist, and the efforts of both to provide their own voluntary schemes of education, made it both more difficult, and less necessary, for the State to intervene. Not until voluntary effort had done what it could, and had discovered that its utmost was not enough, could the aid of the State be finally invoked.

The history of English education is complicated; and the

general development of education in the modern State is more clearly illustrated in France. Under the *ancien régime* education was not a public service; it belonged to the Church and to bodies connected with the Church. Primary education was generally conducted by religious congregations, and especially by the Brothers of the Christian Schools; secondary education, apart from some schools conducted by municipal authorities, belonged to the Jesuits; and the action of the State, confined to the higher ranges of learning, was mainly to be seen in the *Académies* created by Colbert. The practical suppression of the Jesuit Order in France after 1762 was followed by the appearance of a work which constitutes a new epoch—the *Essai d'Éducation Nationale* of La Chalotais (1763). 'I claim for the Nation', he wrote, 'an education dependent upon the State alone, because education belongs essentially to the State; because every nation has an inalienable and imprescriptible right to instruct its members; because, in short, the children of the State should be brought up by those who are members of the State.'[1] The words have had a long echo in France, which has reverberated down to our own times. The Revolutionary leaders, and especially Condorcet, were much occupied by schemes of public education, in which the ideas of *L'École laïque* and of a universal system of compulsory and gratuitous education were prominent features. Napoleon, by a law of 1802, planned a system of State education, which, at any rate, issued in the creation of the French *Lycée*. In the spirit of La Chalotais, he declared that 'unless men are taught from childhood . . . to be republicans or monarchists, Catholics or infidels . . . the State will never make a nation'; and in 1808 he proceeded to institute a central University of France, with a number of local divisions or *Académies*,[2] which he aimed at vesting exclusively with the work of public instruction, and which has continued to survive, in an altered form and with a

---

[1] Quoted in J. W. Adamson, *Short History of Education*, p. 214.

[2] The academies, of which there are seventeen, are the organs of local educational administration, apart from the prefect and the general council of the department. Each has its Rector, its Academic Council, its academy inspector, and its staff of primary inspectors; but it is the prefect of the department, and not the officers of the Academy, who appoints the teachers in the State schools.

different inspiration, to the present time. It is significant that Napoleon concentrated his attention, as France afterwards long continued to do, on the production of an intellectual *élite* and left the work of primary education to the local communes, the Brothers of the Christian Schools, and private enterprise.

The problem of primary education, and of the part which the Church and religious associations should play in its conduct, vexed France for a century after 1815. The tradition of the French Revolution was clear, and it ran in favour of La Chalotais's idea of a system of national education conducted by the State. On the other hand, Napoleon had made a concordat with the Catholic Church in 1802; he had left it still active in primary education; and the monarchy of the Restoration was closely connected with the Church. In 1833, the year in which the English Parliament made its first grant in aid of education, Guizot attempted to solve the problem. Every French commune was to have its school; the Catholic schools were to retain their liberty; the State schools were to be superintended both by the parish priest and by a lay commission drawn from each canton; and the clergy were to collaborate with the officers of the State in promoting 'a system of instruction controlled by religious beliefs'. The third Republic, recurring to the tradition of the Revolution, sought to introduce a national and universal system of State-controlled lay schools. The process was gradual. A law of 1879 instituted *écoles normales primaires* in each department, and thus brought the training of primary teachers within the purview of the State. A law of 1881 made instruction free in all State primary schools, and a law of 1882 made attendance compulsory for all children between the ages of 6 and 13. A further law of 1886 declared that the teachers in State schools should be lay, and at the same time restricted the rights of the Church, both in regard to the superintendence or the inspection of State schools, and in the matter of opening schools of its own. *Liberté d'enseignement*—the right of any citizen, duly qualified, to open a school and to give instruction—continued, and still continues, to be regarded as one of the principles of the Revolution and one of the *droits de l'homme*. But that liberty was definitely

challenged when in 1901 the members of 'unauthorized', and
in 1904 even the members of 'authorized', religious congregations
were forbidden entirely to open schools or to give instruction.
A national system 'dependent upon the State alone' (as La
Chalotais had urged) was thus instituted; and education became,
in the fullest sense of the word, a State service. It was, and is, a
highly centralized service; the appointment of teachers, their
remuneration (which is paid directly by the State), and the
general control of curriculum and instruction, are all vested in
the central government and its local organs. The general system
of French education, until very recent years, has continued to
follow the Napoleonic tradition of concentration upon the training of an intellectual *élite*. Primary education, and the training
of elementary teachers, have been sharply distinguished from
secondary education, which is given largely in the State *lycées*,
and from the training of secondary teachers. But the contemporary development of France, which has now moved towards
free secondary education, is affecting and beginning to obliterate this distinction.

If we attempt to summarize the development of French education, we may say that it has been generally controlled since the
Revolution by the idea of a 'national education' corresponding
to the Revolutionary doctrine of national sovereignty. This idea
has resulted in making education, in the main, an exclusive
State service, not only free from any control by religious bodies,
but also free from any co-operation of religious bodies, such as
our English 'dual' system still retains. The State service of
education, like other State services in France, has followed the
French genius of administrative centralization, and it has been
conducted with a large regard to the production of a class
capable of maintaining the great national tradition of French
culture and civilization. In many respects the development of
France has run ahead of that of England. Guizot was establishing a school in every French commune in the same year in which
the English Parliament was content to vote £20,000 in aid of
voluntary schools; and France established in 1878 a State service
for the training of primary teachers such as England has not

yet provided.[1] On the other hand, a struggle between Church and State such as we have not known has inevitably accompanied the development of education in France. With us, as we shall see, the struggle has been engaged not so much between Church and State as between rival religious bodies—with the State attempting to support both, incurring the accusation that it was supporting only one, and only gradually discovering that it too had its own function, and that it could, and must, discharge a national service of education to its members on its own account.

§ 2. The History of Education in Prussia

In Prussia, to which we may now turn, there has been comparatively little struggle, and a large and fruitful development. Frederick William I, a stern Protestant, was impelled by his religious principles to issue an edict in favour of universal compulsory education soon after 1720, a century and a half before the principle was adopted in England or France. His edict was rather a form of educational conscription than a pledge of State service: he sought to throw the cost of its execution on parents and local communes; and his ambition for an educated Prussia, drilled in religious duty, bore little fruit at the time. Frederick the Great, in 1763, again decreed that all children should attend school between the age of 5 and that of 13, and going beyond his father he sought to aid the poor to meet the cost. His minister Zedlitz, in the latter part of his reign, attempted to found a general State system of education and, though he was compelled to leave primary education to the clergy, he succeeded in bringing secondary and university education under the control of a State department, and in establishing a 'leaving examination' in secondary schools which ultimately became a condition of entry both to the universities and to the ranks of the Prussian administration. The development was continued during the

[1] Since 1902 the local education authorities have founded twenty-two training colleges; but the bulk of our primary teachers are trained in the fifty-four voluntary training colleges and the twenty university training departments. The scheme of a National Normal School, or State Training College, proposed as long ago as 1839, has never been adopted in England.

Prussian Renaissance after the battle of Jena, in the great days when Wilhelm von Humboldt was minister of public instruction, and when the University of Berlin was founded, with Fichte and Niebuhr among its professors, to be the core of the new Prussian spirit (1809).

Already, in 1803, a law containing a 'conscience clause', which permitted parents who had religious objections to withdraw their children from religious instruction based on the principles of the State Church, had gone far to solve the difficulties which had impeded the work of Zedlitz. Already, in 1808, Fichte had spoken in his Addresses to the German nation of the value of the Swiss Pestalozzi's methods as a model which the State might follow in providing for the teaching of the young. A new spirit was brought into primary education; a training college was started in Berlin; and eventually, after study and improvement of the example set by Switzerland, a three years' course was initiated for the training of Prussian schoolmasters. Allenstein, the minister for educational and ecclesiastical affairs after 1815, held the balance even between religious denominations; he pressed forward the erection of elementary schools (founding 400 in the one province of west Prussia in the space of four years); he initiated modern *Realschulen*, in the sphere of secondary education, by the side of the older and more classical *Gymnasia*; and he carried out his reforms, without burdening the finances of the State, by making school expenses a local charge. Universal compulsory education became a fact; and it was conducted as a State service without question or controversy. The Constitution of 1850 enunciated the principle of *liberté d'enseignement*; but education in Prussia (and in Germany at large after the foundation of the Empire in 1871) continued to be provided in State schools. Local authorities—acting in towns by the same method of *ad hoc* committees, enforced by 'special citizens', which was also applied to poor relief—provided school-buildings from local rates; and the State was responsible for providing and paying a body of qualified teachers. The whole scheme of education, from the primary schools and the various forms of secondary school to the universities, was a coherent system controlled by a central ministry; and the benefits of this State system were made more and more accessible to the population at large. The payment of fees was abolished in primary schools; by the beginning of the twentieth century free places or other forms of assistance were being given to some 10 per cent. of the children attending secondary schools; and continuation schools were also being established, in which apprentices and other young workers, after they had completed the stage of primary education at the age of 14, were spending from 6 to 8 hours of their working week. Prussia, which had itself been inspired by Swiss example in the first decade of the nineteenth century, became an inspiration to England; and German methods of State education, like German methods of social insurance, affected the course of English development.

§ 3. *Education in England before and after 1832*

Prussia was thus first in the field[1] in establishing a compulsory system of national education—a system which has been called 'the straitest of State school systems', but which, at the same time, was also the most comprehensive and generous in the service which it rendered to all the members of the community.

It was the good fortune of Prussia that she escaped the struggle

---

[1] In Prussia the principle of universal compulsory education was already affirmed two centuries ago by Frederick William I, and reaffirmed, in 1763, by Frederick the Great's *Landschulregiment*; and it was made effective by the work of von Humboldt and Allenstein in the early years of the nineteenth century. The Scottish system of parochial schools, with its different inspiration, is as old as 1696. In England the principle of universal compulsory education was introduced in 1881; in France, in 1882; and in Italy (but only from the age of 6 to that of 9) in 1877. It should be added, however, that there was a general interest in education in most of the German States during the latter half of the eighteenth century. Maria Theresa had already begun to reform education in Austria by 1760, and when the Jesuit Order was suppressed by the Bull *Dominus ac Redemptor* in 1773, she used the funds and buildings of the Order, which had been used for secondary instruction, in order to create elementary schools and training colleges (1774). Joseph II, who proclaimed that 'the State is no cloister', and issued a Patent of Tolerance in favour of all Christian denominations in 1781, extended his mother's policy, and even attempted to bring the seminaries for the education of the clergy under the authority of the State. His successors, inspired by the legitimist reaction against the Revolution, and returning to the old Austrian alliance with the Church, deserted the policy which Joseph had pursued, and into which he had drawn his mother in the later years of her reign.

between Church and State which long troubled France; it was equally her good fortune that she escaped the rivalry of different denominations which long vexed the development of English education. In England the history of education, down to the Reform Bill of 1832, and even afterwards, may be said to be a chapter in the history of the Church of England and especially of its relations with the Nonconformist Churches.

The bishop, under the Elizabethan system, was the educational authority who licensed teachers. Education was regarded as the office of the Church and the duty of its schoolmasters (who were, if possible, according to the canons of 1604, to be beneficed clergymen); and its aim was conceived to be the securing of religious uniformity in a Christian commonwealth whose members all belonged, or should duly be trained to belong, to the Church established by law. The Rebellion of 1641, and the victory of the Puritans, gave a temporary triumph to a very different set of ideas. The Czech educationalist, Comenius, who advocated a State system of education, with universal compulsory elementary instruction, was invited to England; Samuel Hartlib, a Pole who had come to England in 1628 and had become the friend of Milton (himself the author of a tractate *On Education*), popularized his principles in pamphlets; and English authors, such as William Petty, ancestor of the fortunes of the Lansdowne family, advocated similar ideas. The Long Parliament, like the French Revolutionary assemblies after 1789, debated schemes of public education; but the one result was a parliamentary grant in 1649 of £20,000 from the confiscated property of the Church (the amount, by a curious coincidence, is the same as that voted by Parliament in 1833), of which £18,000 was to be applied to the maintenance of ministers and schoolmasters—the rest going to increase the salaries of heads of houses in Oxford and Cambridge.

The idea of supplanting clerical control of education by a system of State schools perished with the restoration of the Anglican Church in 1660. The Act of Uniformity (1662) tightened episcopal control of education; and the Conventicle and Five Mile Acts (1664 and 1665) forbade Nonconformists to teach. The English system of parliamentary government began its history in 1660 with the principle that the State, as such, had no interest in education, and should simply confer a monopoly of control upon the State Church. The practice was in some respects better than the principle. By a tacit compromise which went beyond the limits of the law, Nonconformists were not only allowed to teach, but to open 'academies' for their members, and an Act of Parliament in 1779 gave legal sanction to the practice. But if the monopoly of the State Church was thus removed, the fundamental idea survived that education was the function of religious bodies, and not of the State. During the greater part of the eighteenth century, while Nonconformity still laboured under legal disabilities, and before the Wesleyan movement had vastly increased the number of its adherents, the duty of education fell mainly upon the State Church. It sought to perform that duty, from 1699 to 1760, by a system of charity schools,[1] managed by the Society for the Promotion of Christian Knowledge. The system was characteristic, in two respects, of a trend which long affected the history of English education. It remitted elementary instruction to the care of a voluntary society; and it devolved the cost of such instruction upon charitable subscriptions, contributed by the richer class for the improvement of the labouring poor by means of a training in religious knowledge and useful arts.

The movement in favour of the charity school had spent its force by 1760; and for a time there was a lull. While the Continent was being stirred, first by the suppression of the Jesuit Order after 1760 and the ideas of State education which that suppression evoked, and afterwards by the revolutionary principle of national sovereignty and its corollary of the right of the sovereign nation to be educated, England remained unstirred. No party in the State would subscribe to the dangerous doctrine

---

[1] The charity schools were not the first elementary schools in England. 'Petty schools', preparatory to the 'grammar' or secondary school, are already to be found in the sixteenth century, and increased in number in the seventeenth. But the charity schools, with the S.P.C.K. in London acting as a sort of board of education, and with the local trustees who managed the schools assuming the position of a local education authority, were the first general system.

of a system of national education given and controlled by the State. To the Nonconformist, as Priestley wrote in 1768, 'education was a branch of civil liberty which ought by no means to be surrendered into the hands of the civil magistrate'; he felt that the only way of preserving the balance between political and religious parties was that 'each party should provide for the education of their own children'.[1] To the Anglican, education was an office and duty of the clergy; and if he was now ready to concede to the Nonconformists what he had once claimed exclusively for himself, he was far from being ready to resign to the State a right which would menace his Church. There was thus a general agreement, which radicals such as William Godwin, the author of *Political Justice*, could share with the Anglican clergy, that a system of national education would threaten the liberty of all Englishmen by strengthening unduly the powers of government. In the strength of this belief all parties set to work 'to provide for the education of their own children' by their own efforts. The first result was the system of Sunday schools, which played a great part in England during the fifty years after the foundation of the Sunday Schools Union in 1785. Organized by all the denominations, these schools were primarily intended to teach young children, from the age of 8 to that of 12, to read the Bible on Sunday; but they soon came to teach during the evenings of the week as well as on Sundays, and to provide instruction in writing and arithmetic, and sometimes in other subjects, as well as in English. As late as 1835 they could still be counted as perhaps the most valuable and the most effective organ of popular instruction.

By that time, however, voluntary effort had added a third organ to the old charity schools of the first half and the Sunday Schools of the later years of the eighteenth century. This was the voluntary day-school, in the form in which it was developed, about 1810, by two new voluntary educational societies—the National Society, which founded schools for the children of Anglican parents, and the British and Foreign School Society,

[1] Quoted in Adamson, op. cit., pp. 216–17.

which founded schools for the children of Nonconformists. There ensued a period of more or less amicable rivalry, in which the competitors were concerned to anticipate and outstrip the advent of a system of State education, while the State itself was content for long years to be left out of the running. But the attempt to construct a national scheme of education on the basis of voluntary contributions by different religious bodies was necessarily doomed to failure. Appealing to the charitable instincts of their supporters, both societies were compelled to plead that they existed 'for the education of the poor'; and they were thus condemned by their nature to perpetuate an old English tradition, unsuited to a new democratic age, that education was a charity rather than a right.[1] Nor were voluntary subscriptions, on whatever ground they were solicited, and however liberally they were given, adequate to the task of providing education for an industrialized country which was increasing its population by leaps and bounds. Both societies, indeed, attempted to reduce to a minimum the cost of the instruction which they provided by employing a monitorial system, under which the elder pupils taught the younger, and the payment of salaries to teachers became almost unnecessary. But the expedient was a poor thing in comparison with the Prussian system of trained schoolmasters; and the expense of providing the necessary school-buildings still remained.

A new system was obviously necessary, in which education would be provided for all as a right, and not for 'the Poor' as a charity, and in which the cost would be borne by all, through the payment of rates and taxes, and not by the few who were able and willing to pay voluntary contributions. Slowly England resigned itself to the necessity of a State service of education financed, like other State services, from the funds of the State. In this respect, as in so many others (the history of poor relief, for example, and the general history of English administration), the Reform Bill of 1832 marked an epoch. Just as the Revolu-

---

[1] The National Society styled itself a society 'for promoting the education of the Poor in the principles of the Church of England'. The British Society, which began with the efforts of Joseph Lancaster, was originally termed 'the Royal British or Lancastrian system for the education of the Poor'.

tionary doctrine of *souveraineté nationale* entailed the education of the national Sovereign, so the 'Representation of the People Act', as its legal title ran, involved the education of the enfranchised People. As early as 1833 Roebuck, the member for Bath, recognized the logic of events, and introduced a motion in favour of universal and compulsory instruction controlled by a Ministry of Education.[1] Parliament, still clinging to the voluntary system, and still prepared to confine its view to the poor, was content to vote an annual grant of £20,000 'in aid of private subscriptions . . . for the education of the poorer classes'. It was a little seed; but it germinated rapidly. In 1839 a Committee of the Privy Council on Education was instituted to superintend the application of the grant; and Sir James Kay-Shuttleworth became its first secretary. Education thus found a place in the administrative system; and with that place secured, Kay-Shuttleworth was able (exactly like his contemporary Chadwick in the parallel field of poor relief and local government) to develop a scheme of educational inspection and administration which was the necessary basis of future progress. By 1856 an Education Department had been formed; by 1858 (a quarter of a century after the first grant) Parliament was voting £663,000 per annum; and in the same year a Royal Commission was appointed to report on 'the extension of . . . elementary instruction to all classes of the people'.[2]

It would be a grave error to assume that, because England was slow in adopting a State system of education, she was oblivious to the need of education itself, or had failed to make provision for meeting the need. On the contrary, the voluntary subscriptions given in aid of education were remarkable; they amounted, in 1858, to double the amount of the grant made by the State; and that had been their average amount since 1833. But a system under which the State provided neither schools nor

[1] Roebuck was nearly fifty years ahead of his time in pleading for universal compulsory education, and nearly seventy in advocating a Ministry of Education.

[2] The width of the terms of reference is perhaps significant. It imports a recognition of the principle that education is a service owed to the whole community, simply because, as Huxley said, 'they are men and women', and not to a class because it is poor.

teachers itself, but only aided voluntary bodies to make such provision, could not meet the needs of a population which had risen, between 1831 and 1871, from fourteen millions to nearly twenty-three. By the Education Act of 1870 Parliament took a final step; it added a new system of State schools to the old voluntary system, and it committed the administration of these schools to a new organ of local government called the School Board. A dual system was thus founded, which placed the State (or 'Board') schools by the side of the voluntary schools created by the various denominational societies. Religious instruction was to be given in the State schools, but it was to be un-denominational; and parents were permitted, by a conscience clause, to withdraw their children from such instruction. On this dual basis, by virtue of the English genius for a clumsy com-promise which is somehow made to work, the general system of elementary education has since continued to rest. The State has ceased to aid the erection of voluntary schools; it has left them in existence (indeed the number of voluntary schools is still greater than that of State schools); and by the Education Act of 1902 it even permitted them to be aided from local rates in meeting the cost of the instruction—other than religious—which they provide.

The Act of 1870 did not introduce compulsory elementary education, though it empowered each school board to require attendance by passing a by-law to that effect. A new Act of 1880, which came into force in 1881, introduced universal com-pulsion; a further Act of 1891 made elementary education 'free'. In 1900 the old Committee of the Privy Council on Education became a Board of Education, under a President of its own who has as a rule a seat in the Cabinet. Education was thus estab-lished as a public service, with its own place in the government of the country as well as in the administrative system; and on this basis a further advance was made by the Act of 1902. The local control of education was taken from the school boards, and entrusted to the elected councils of counties and boroughs, acting through education committees which contained co-opted members; and the province of the new local authorities was extended to include the provision of secondary education,[1] to which the most promising of the children in primary schools were freely admitted by a system of scholarships and free places. The Act was a landmark in several respects. It extended the system of State education from the primary to the secondary stage; it extended the right to education, by providing a new door of opportunity through which children might pass from the free primary school, by means of scholarships or other assistance, to the secondary school and the university; and it reformed the administration of education by constituting strong local authorities, with administrative staffs of their own, which have gradually come to 'balance', in the traditional English way, the central authority—or rather to co-operate with it under a system of State grants in aid of local expenditure.

The last thirty years, if they can show no great or particular landmark, have been filled by many new growths, as if England were resolved that when movement had once begun it should be both rapid and general. Seven of the English universities have been founded, in their present form, since 1900; and the State has extended its system of grants to aid all the universities of Great Britain. The primary schools are being reformed at both ends—on the one hand by a movement towards nursery and infant schools, and on the other by a policy of instituting central schools, to which all children who do not go forward to secondary schools are to be transferred at the age of 11. Training colleges for teachers have been founded by the new local education authorities; and these, along with the old voluntary training colleges, have been brought into closer connexion with the universities. A new movement for adult education has been started by the Workers Educational Association; and this movement, with the aid of the universities and of the State, has provided tutorial classes for urban workers, and is now spreading into rural villages. The ardent reformer may sadly reflect on 'the petty done, the undone vast'; but on a long view we cannot

[1] But boroughs which are not 'county boroughs' (i.e. boroughs equal to counties, and therefore independent of the authority of the county in which they are situated) are only competent to deal with elementary education; and the county authority therefore controls secondary education within their area.

but recognize that the Modern State is steadily moving, in education as in other matters, towards a higher conception of the services which it must render, and the rights which it must guarantee, to its members. If, in the sphere of its 'social services' proper, it is adopting the principle of welfare, we may also say that, in its educational service, it is adopting the ideal of an 'education of humanity' which runs from the nursery school to the adult tutorial class. Isocrates once said of his country, in one of his speeches, that 'Hellas had become a *paideia*'—an education and a culture. The Modern State will perhaps always remain an 'economy' as well as a *paideia*, and it will long continue to be concerned with the material cares of its great household no less than with the spiritual growth of all its members. But at any rate we may say, at the end of this review, that the Modern State has travelled a long way, since 1660, towards a conception of its services which will include mind as well as body, and spiritual development as well as material welfare.

One other thing may also be said. When we consider the history of the Modern State, not only in education, but in all its services and activities, we cannot but recognize the debt which all States owe to one another. Each country has developed according to its own genius; and each has produced its own fruit. But each has produced some institution, or some method of public service, which has served as an example to others; and each, in turn, has borrowed from each. There has been a rivalry of methods, but it has not been unfriendly; one country has studied, adopted, or tried to improve the methods of another; and all have combined, however unconsciously, to promote the growth of a common European standard of administration and public service.